MAIN-COURSE SANDWICHES

MAIN-COURSE SANDWICHES

RAY OVERTON

PHOTOGRAPHS BY BRAD NEWTON

LONGSTREET
Atlanta, Georgia

*This book is dedicated with love and respect
to Nathalie Dupree, my mentor, teacher, colleague, and friend.
Thank you for my career!*

Published by
LONGSTREET PRESS, INC.
A subsidiary of Cox Newspapers,
A subsidiary of Cox Enterprises, Inc.
2140 Newmarket Parkway
Suite 122
Marietta, GA 30067

Printed in Hong Kong by Paramount Printing
1st printing, 1999
Library of Congress Catalog Card Number: 99-61760
ISBN: 1-56352-576-3

Book and jacket design by Burtch Bennett Hunter

Visit Longstreet on the World Wide Web
www.lspress.com

CONTENTS

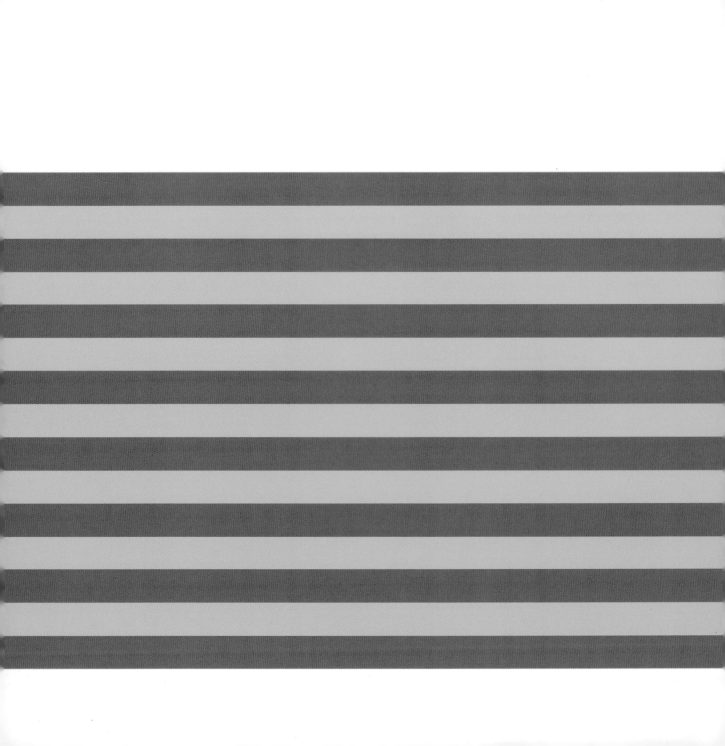

INTRODUCTION

Sandwiches, like old friends, need very little introduction. Almost everyone in the world has eaten some form of a sandwich — sliced meats or vegetables wrapped in a baked grain product. Essentially, sandwiches have been around as long as that cornerstone of our diet, bread. After all, no matter what Miss Manners says, a piece of bread serves as the perfect scoop for other foods.

The sandwich is thought to be named after John Montagu, the Fourth Earl of Sandwich. As the story goes, Montagu was such a passionate and prolific gambler that he would often send his servants to fetch him cold sliced meat between two slices of bread so that he would not have to leave his place at the gaming tables to satisfy his hunger. That makes the name quite recent in the evolution of things, dating from the beginning of the nineteenth century, but the practice of eating meats encased in bread slices is ancient history. In feudal times, laborers in the field were traditionally fed a meal of roasted meats and bread (mostly bread with very little meat, often on the verge of rancidity and slathered in gravy to hide or disguise the taste of the reeking meat itself). On a more pleasant note, medieval travelers on their pilgrimages from one place to the next could easily tote this life-sustaining nourishment in their packs.

Main-Course Sandwiches seemed a natural addition to my *Main-Course* series because it so much exemplifies my cooking philosophy — that is, the layering of flavor upon flavor, unique tastes, textures, and aromas of varying ingredients, all building one on the other to create a finished dish that is more than the sum of its parts. These resulting sandwich creations are full-flavored, delicious, and reasonably uncomplicated. There is no reason to settle for the common, everyday, traditional forms of the sandwich — unless that's truly what your heart desires.

I have divided the recipes in this book into six chapters:

1 Picnic Sandwiches are make-ahead creations that lend themselves to being easily packed and transported.

2 Party Sandwiches are those designed to help you celebrate fun and festive occasions throughout the year. (Yes, sandwiches are appropriate for entertaining. There's something very communal about enjoying foods we pick up with our hands and eat.)

3 Fast and Flavorful Sandwiches are those perfect for a busy lifestyle. They are quick and easy meals — ready in 30 minutes or less — yet still full of flavor. Also, you can eat these sandwiches on the go. (Some may necessitate a couple more napkins than others.)

4 Contemporary Classic Sandwiches are the old favorites that have withstood the test of time, updated for today's more sophisticated palate.

5 International Sandwiches and Burgers are world-renowned choices that combine influences from a global kitchen, using ingredients of varying origins and cuisines.

6 Sandwich Spreads, Relishes, and Toppings is probably the most useful chapter in this book. I consider all the recipes I write to be merely blueprints, a foundation to get you started. This final chapter, along with the variations at the end of each sandwich recipe, allows you to mix and

match, create, experiment, sample, and savor a variety of tastes and textures by substituting different meats, cheeses, breads, vegetables, spreads, salsas, relishes, and toppings.

In my opinion, it is the condiment that gives the sandwich its unique flavor and character. Change it and you dramatically alter the taste of the dish. One of the most fun parts about putting this book together was experimenting with the various condiments to see in what directions I could take the overall taste of the sandwich. I am sure I only scratched the surface. It is now your chance to get creative, to make these recipes your own. You alone know what you, your family, and your friends prefer, so I'm making it official: You have my permission to relax and have fun in the kitchen, but be a little daring, too, and then enjoy the fruits of your labor with those you love.

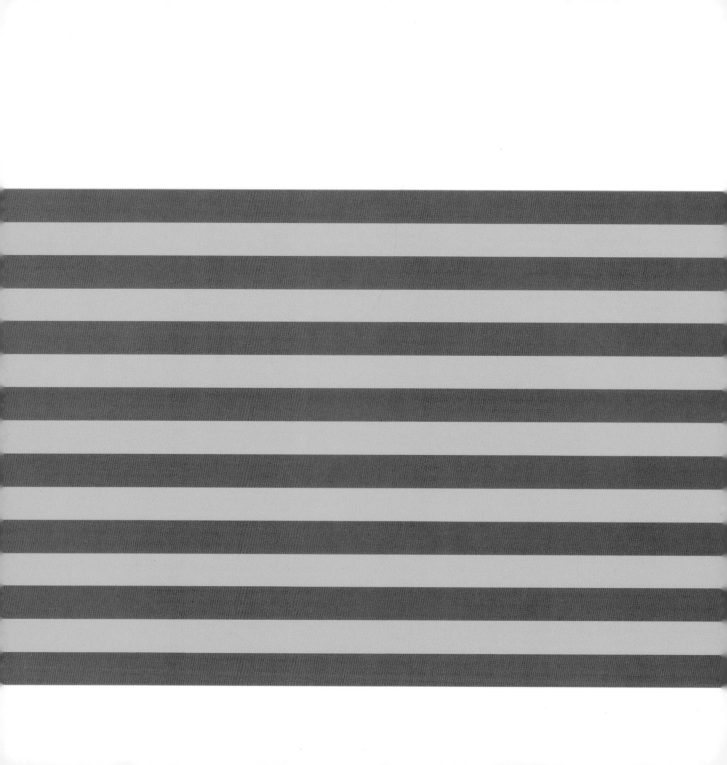

PICNIC
SANDWICHES

The Ultimate Muffuletta

Toasted Ham and Havarti Sandwich

Spicy Malaysian Chicken Salad Sandwich

Super Summertime Stuffed Sandwich

Roast Beef Triple Decker Sandwich

Deviled Ham Salad Croissant

Smoked Salmon, Fennel, and Cream Cheese Bagel

Italian Hero Sandwich

Pan Bagnat

Poached Salmon Salad Sandwich

THE ULTIMATE MUFFULETTA

This delicious New Orleans specialty originated in 1906 in the city's Central Grocery. It is the olive relish, or tapenade, that sets it apart. Weighting the sandwich overnight allows the flavors to mingle, thus creating a compact, easy-to-hold, eat-on-the-go wedge of tastes and textures.

SERVES 8

1 large round loaf Italian bread (about 10 inches in diameter)

1 cup Black Olive Tapenade (see page 104)

2 cups mesclun (mixed baby greens)

6 ounces thinly sliced mortadella or other soft salami

4 ounces thinly sliced fontina cheese

6 ounces thinly sliced sopressata or other hard salami

4 ounces thinly sliced provolone cheese

4 plum tomatoes, thinly sliced

3 ounces thinly sliced pepperoni

1 red onion, thinly sliced

½ cup freshly grated Parmesan cheese

Freshly ground black pepper

1 cup Green Olive Tapenade (see page 114)

With a serrated knife split the Italian loaf in half horizontally. Remove most of the soft inside bread, creating a cavity inside each half.

Spread the Black Olive Tapenade evenly inside the bottom half. Arrange half of the mesclun on the bottom bread half, then layer the mortadella, fontina, sopressata, provolone, plum tomatoes, pepperoni, and red onion. Top with the remaining mesclun and sprinkle with the Parmesan cheese. Season to taste with freshly ground black pepper.

Spread the Green Olive Tapenade inside the cavity of the upper bread half. Carefully place on top of the layered half and press down. Wrap tightly with plastic wrap. Place the sandwich on a large baking sheet and cover with another baking sheet. Weight the top baking sheet with 3 to 4 pounds of canned goods or 2 bricks wrapped in foil. Refrigerate for 8 hours or overnight.

To serve, unwrap the loaf and cut into 8 wedges. Serve chilled or at room temperature.

Variations: For the olive tapenades, substitute Roasted Red Bell Pepper Tapenade, Garlic Mayonnaise (Aioli), Traditional Italian Pesto, or Sun-Dried Tomato Pesto. You can also omit the tomatoes and red onion and substitute Mediterranean Artichoke Salsa or the Marinated Mushroom Salsa.

TOASTED HAM & HAVARTI SANDWICH

⊳—◂◆▸—◇—◂◆▸—◃

A spicy pear chutney gives this savory sandwich a burst of flavor. The chutney perfectly accents many different meats and cheeses so feel free to experiment. You can substitute turkey and Swiss, roast beef and cheddar, or grilled pork tenderloin and Gruyère for the ham and Havarti cheese. It is absolutely delicious every time!

SERVES 4

8 slices dark pumpernickel rye bread, toasted

¼ cup Dijon mustard

1 cup Pear and Golden Raisin Chutney (see page 107)

12 ounces thinly sliced hickory-smoked ham

8 ounces thinly sliced Havarti cheese

Spread each slice of the toasted pumpernickel rye bread with Dijon mustard. Spread about ¼ cup of the Pear and Golden Raisin Chutney on 4 slices of bread. Layer with the sliced ham and Havarti. Top each sandwich with the second slice of bread. Slice on the diagonal and serve.

These sandwiches can be made up to 6 hours ahead, tightly wrapped with plastic wrap, and stored in the refrigerator. Serve chilled or at room temperature. Pass the remaining chutney separately if desired.

Variation: Substitute Fresh Cranberry Orange Relish or Vidalia Onion Marmalade for the chutney.

SPICY MALAYSIAN CHICKEN SALAD SANDWICH

⋈—⬦—⋈

Malaya, one of my favorite restaurants in Atlanta, serves Acar (pronounced "a-CHA") as an appetizer. I have adapted this spicy pickle salad to use as the base for this unusual chicken salad recipe. Beware . . . it is fiery hot — a real eye-opener. For milder palates reduce the amount of chili garlic paste and chili oil in the Acar.

SERVES 8

2½ cups Acar (see page 109)

4 cups shredded cooked chicken

1 head radicchio lettuce, separated into leaves

8 large whole-wheat pitas, split horizontally

1 cup alfalfa sprouts, for garnish

With a slotted spoon remove the vegetables from the Acar and mix in a large bowl with the shredded chicken. Place 1 radicchio lettuce leaf into each pita half. Fill the pita with the chicken salad mixture. Top with alfalfa sprouts. Serve at once at room temperature, passing the dressing from the Acar separately.

Variation: Substitute a double recipe of Asian Peanut Sauce for the Acar. Omit the alfalfa sprouts and top with fresh pineapple chunks and crunchy chow mein noodles.

Note: To take this sandwich on a picnic, pack the chicken and Acar separately. Mix and fill the pita pockets just before serving.

9

SUPER SUMMERTIME STUFFED SANDWICH

This is the vegetarian version of the Ultimate Muffuletta. For a smoky taste, grill the vegetables over red-hot hardwood coals on an outdoor barbecue.

SERVES 8

1 large eggplant, cut into ½-inch thick rounds

2 zucchini, cut into ½-inch thick rounds

2 yellow squash, cut into ½-inch thick rounds

1 large Vidalia onion, cut into ½-inch thick rounds

1 cup Garlic Herb Vinaigrette (see page 112)

Salt and freshly ground black pepper

1 cup freshly grated Parmesan cheese

1 large round loaf Italian bread (about 10 inches in diameter)

2 cups mesclun (mixed baby greens)

6 ounces crumbled feta cheese

8 ounces Brie or Camembert cheese, rind intact, softened, sliced lengthwise into ¼-inch thick slices

1 cup tightly packed fresh basil leaves

4 plum tomatoes, thinly sliced

Preheat the oven to 425° F. Place the sliced eggplant, zucchini, squash, and onion on 2 large baking sheets coated with nonstick cooking spray. Brush the vegetables with half of the Garlic Herb Vinaigrette. Season generously with salt and pepper. Roast in the oven about 20 minutes, rotating the pans halfway through the cooking time. Remove from the oven and sprinkle with the Parmesan cheese.

With a serrated knife split the Italian loaf in half horizontally. Remove most of the interior bread. Brush each bread cavity with the remaining vinaigrette. Cover the bottom half with half of the mesclun, then the eggplant, feta cheese, zucchini, Brie or Camembert cheese, squash, basil leaves, tomatoes, and the remaining mesclun. Season to taste with freshly ground black pepper.

Press the top half of the bread onto the layered half. Wrap tightly with plastic wrap. Place the sandwich on a large baking sheet and cover with another baking sheet. Weight the top baking sheet with 3 to 4 pounds of canned goods or 2 bricks wrapped in foil. Refrigerate for 8 hours or overnight. To serve, unwrap the loaf and cut into 8 wedges. Serve chilled or at room temperature.

Variation: Omit the vinaigrette. Brush the vegetable slices with ½ cup extra-virgin olive oil and roast as directed. Brush the bread cavities with olive oil. In place of the zucchini, spread about 1 cup of Mediterranean Artichoke Salsa or Marinated Mushroom Salsa in between the cheeses when assembling the layers.

ROAST BEEF TRIPLE DECKER SANDWICH

This sandwich reminds me of one of Dagwood's late-night, raid-the-refrigerator creations from the Sunday comics. It certainly takes Goliath's mouth to get around one of them, but it is well worth the effort.

MAKES 4 SANDWICHES

⅔ cup Horseradish and Caper Mayonnaise (see page 106)

8 slices seven-grain bread, toasted

¼ cup coarse-grained Dijon mustard

4 slices white bread, toasted

12 ounces thinly sliced rare roast beef

16 sliced bread-and-butter pickles

1 Belgian endive, separated into individual spears

2 tomatoes, thinly sliced

2 avocados, peeled and sliced

1 lemon, cut into 4 wedges

Salt and freshly ground black pepper

16 pimiento-stuffed green olives, skewered with toothpicks

Spread the Horseradish and Caper Mayonnaise evenly on one side of each seven-grain bread slice. Lightly spread the Dijon mustard on both sides of each white bread slice.

Top 4 of the seven-grain bread slices with the roast beef. Top the beef with the bread-and-butter pickles and Belgian endive. Cover this layer with the white bread, then arrange the tomatoes and avocado slices on top. Squeeze a wedge of lemon over each sandwich. Season to taste with salt and freshly ground black pepper. Top with the remaining slices of seven-grain bread. Press together slightly and then cut each sandwich into 4 quarters. Secure each sandwich quarter with an olive-skewered toothpick.

Variation: Herbed Honey Mustard, Curried Mayonnaise, Garlic Mayonnaise (Aioli), or Gorgonzola Cream Cheese Spread makes a nice substitute for the Horseradish and Caper Mayonnaise.

11

DEVILED HAM SALAD CROISSANT

In savory culinary terms, "deviled" refers to a food that is mixed with a hot or spicy flavoring such as Tabasco, curry powder, or cayenne pepper. When making the Curried Mayonnaise for this recipe, toast the curry powder in a dry skillet. That allows the many dry spices in this unique seasoning blend to develop a more distinct taste and aroma.

SERVES 8

4 cups chopped cooked ham

1 rib of celery, chopped

3 green onions, chopped

1 (10 ounce) package frozen chopped spinach, defrosted and squeezed dry

⅔ cup Curried Mayonnaise (see page 116)

½ teaspoon Tabasco

Salt and freshly ground black pepper

8 large sandwich croissants, split in half horizontally

1 small head frisée lettuce, tough outer leaves discarded

2 star fruit, sliced, optional

In a large bowl combine the chopped ham, celery, green onions, spinach, Curried Mayonnaise, Tabasco, and salt and pepper to taste.

Divide the frisée and optional star fruit among the 8 bottom halves of the croissants. Then divide and spread the deviled ham and top with the second croissant halves. These sandwiches can be made up to 6 hours ahead, tightly wrapped with plastic wrap, and refrigerated. Serve chilled or at room temperature.

Variation: Substitute Garlic Mayonnaise (Aioli), Cilantro and Chipotle Pepper Pesto, or Hot Jalapeño Mustard (plus ¼ cup mayonnaise) for the Curried Mayonnaise.

SMOKED SALMON, FENNEL, & CREAM CHEESE BAGEL

Jewish immigrants first introduced bagels into the United States. These dense, doughnut-shaped yeast rolls with their chewy interior and shiny crust are ideal vehicles for various sandwich fillings. They achieve their characteristic chewiness by being boiled in water before they are baked.

MAKES **4** SANDWICHES

4 plain or onion bagels, split and toasted

1 cup Caper and Green Peppercorn Cream Cheese Spread (see page 111)

8 ounces thinly sliced smoked salmon

1 fennel bulb, cored and thinly sliced

1 small red onion, thinly sliced

Salt and freshly ground black pepper

Fresh dill sprigs for garnish

Spread the Caper and Green Peppercorn Cream Cheese evenly over the bagel halves.

Arrange the smoked salmon over the 4 bottom halves. Top with the fennel and red onion slices. Season to taste with salt and freshly ground black pepper and garnish with the fresh sprigs of dill. Cover each with the top bagel half and press lightly. Cut in half, if desired. These bagel sandwiches can be made up to 4 hours ahead, tightly wrapped with plastic wrap, and stored in the refrigerator.

Variation: Substitute one cup of Dilled Tartar Sauce or Raita Cucumber Sauce for the Caper and Green Peppercorn Cream Cheese Spread. Flaked smoked trout or mackerel makes a nice alternative to the smoked salmon.

ITALIAN HERO SANDWICH

Whether you call it a hero, bomber, grinder, submarine, wedge, zep, or hoagie, any good Italian delicatessen will be able to supply the meats, peppers, cheeses, and crusty bread for this whole meal deal. It is basically a smorgasbord on a bun, so use whatever suits your individual tastes.

SERVES 4

1 large loaf (about 24 inches long) Italian bread, sliced horizontally

1 cup Traditional Italian Pesto (see page 112)

½ small head iceberg lettuce, thinly sliced (about 2 cups)

1 small red onion, thinly sliced

4 plum tomatoes, thinly sliced

6 ounces thinly sliced Genoa salami

6 ounces thinly sliced bologna

6 ounces thinly sliced olive loaf

6 ounces thinly sliced prosciutto ham

8 ounces thinly sliced provolone or mozzarella cheese

½ cup seeded and chopped pepperoncini

½ cup seeded and chopped cherry peppers

½ cup pitted kalamata olives

⅓ cup balsamic vinegar

Salt and freshly ground black pepper

Spread the Traditional Italian Pesto inside both halves of the Italian loaf. On the bottom half, layer the iceberg lettuce, red onion, plum tomatoes, Genoa salami, bologna, olive loaf, prosciutto ham, provolone or mozzarella cheese, pepperoncini, cherry peppers, and kalamata olives. Drizzle with balsamic vinegar and season with salt and freshly ground black pepper to taste. Top with the other half of the Italian loaf. Enclose in plastic wrap and refrigerate at least 6 hours to allow the flavors to develop.

To serve, unwrap the loaf and slice on the diagonal into four 6-inch portions.

Variation: Try using Sun-Dried Tomato Pesto, Roasted Red Bell Pepper Tapenade, or Mayonnaise with Fresh Herbs instead of the Traditional Italian Pesto.

PAN BAGNAT

>+>—O—<+<

Pan Bagnat (pronounced pan-ban-YAH), literally meaning "bathed bread," is an easy-to-hold sandwich popular in the South of France at picnics and outdoor cafés. When you weight the sandwich, the bread absorbs the vinaigrette, making every bite moist and flavorful.

1 large French baguette (about 24 inches long)

1 cup Garlic Herb Vinaigrette (see page 112)

1 cup tightly packed fresh basil leaves

1 red onion, thinly sliced

1 red bell pepper, seeded and sliced into rings

1 green bell pepper, seeded and sliced into rings

4 plum tomatoes, thinly sliced

3 hard-cooked eggs, peeled and sliced

1 (2 ounce) can flat anchovy fillets, drained

1 (6 ounce) can oil-packed tuna, preferably albacore, drained

½ cup pitted niçoise or kalamata olives

¼ cup capers

½ cup freshly grated Parmesan cheese

Salt and freshly ground black pepper

Split the French baguette in half horizontally without cutting all the way through the opposite crust. Open the baguette and brush with half of the Garlic Herb Vinaigrette.

Arrange the basil leaves, red onion, red bell pepper, green bell pepper, plum tomatoes, egg slices, anchovies, tuna, olives, capers, and Parmesan cheese on the bottom half of the bread. Drizzle with the remaining vinaigrette and season to taste with salt and pepper. Close the baguette firmly.

Wrap tightly in plastic wrap, place it on a large baking sheet, and cover with another baking sheet. Weight the top baking sheet with 3 to 4 pounds of canned goods or 2 bricks wrapped in foil. Refrigerate for at least 6 hours to allow the dressing to soak into the bread. To serve, unwrap the loaf and slice diagonally into 4 equal portions.

Variation: Any commercial Italian salad dressing can be substituted for the Garlic Herb Vinaigrette, as well as Mayonnaise with Fresh Herbs, Traditional Italian Pesto, or Sun-Dried Tomato Pesto.

POACHED SALMON SALAD SANDWICH

Poaching is by far the easiest way to keep fish fillets moist and flavorful. This delectable fish salad sandwich mixes poached salmon with Raita, an Indian yogurt-based sauce designed to offer a cooling counterpoint to spicy dishes — creating a unique transportable feast. For a Southwestern sandwich, omit the eggs, red onion, red bell pepper, serrano chiles, and cilantro in the recipe and use Tomatillo and Green Chile Salsa or Salsa Fresca. Wrap the mixture in warmed flour tortillas and sprinkle with 1 cup shredded cheddar cheese.

MAKES 6 SANDWICHES

1 small onion, sliced

4 parsley sprigs

1 lemon, sliced

10 black peppercorns

3 whole eggs in the shell

6 (6 ounce) boneless, skinless salmon fillets

1 red bell pepper, seeded and chopped

1 small red onion, chopped

1 serrano chile, seeded and finely chopped

2 cups Raita Cucumber Sauce (see page 107)

12 (1-inch thick) slices challah bread, toasted

6 leaves red-leaf lettuce

Salt and freshly ground black pepper

⅓ cup fresh cilantro leaves

In a 5½-quart Dutch oven place the onion, parsley, lemon, peppercorns, and whole eggs. Add enough water to fill the Dutch oven halfway. Bring to a boil, reduce the heat to a simmer, and gently nestle the salmon fillets in the water. Cover and cook until the salmon flakes easily with a fork, about 10 minutes per inch of thickness. Remove fillets and drain on paper towels. Remove the eggs and peel under cold running water. Coarsely chop the hard-cooked eggs.

In a large bowl flake the salmon into bite-sized pieces with 2 forks. Add the chopped eggs, red bell pepper, red onion, serrano chile, and the Raita Cucumber Sauce. Toss to mix completely.

To assemble the sandwiches place the lettuce leaves on 6 of the toasted challah slices. Divide and spread the salmon salad on top of the lettuce, season to taste with salt and pepper, and scatter the cilantro leaves on top. Cover with the second piece of toasted bread. These sandwiches can be made up to 4 hours ahead, tightly wrapped with plastic wrap, and refrigerated.

Variation: Dilled Tartar Sauce, Spicy Cocktail Sauce, or Avocado and Yogurt Sauce makes a nice alternative to the Raita.

18

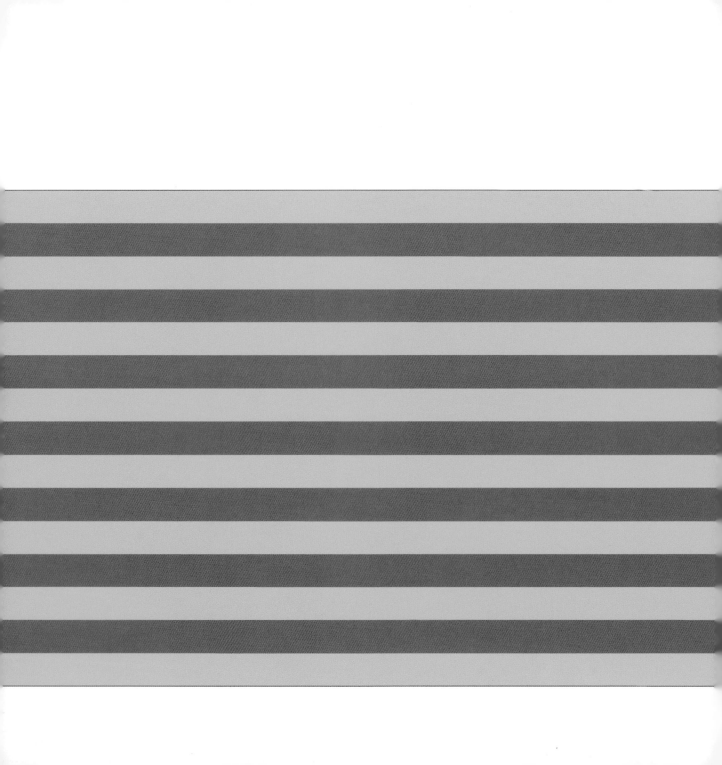

PARTY SANDWICHES

Savory Chopped Pork with Twelve Oaks Barbecue Sauce

Hearty Reuben Loaf

New England Lobster Roll

Mediterranean Braided Bread

Citrus-Glazed Pork Buns

Herb-Rubbed Beef Tenderloin with Jicama Coleslaw

Ratatouille on Sun-Dried Tomato Focaccia

Fiesta Cornmeal Taco Ring

Philadelphia Cheese Steak

SAVORY CHOPPED PORK WITH TWELVE OAKS BARBECUE SAUCE

This recipe has been adapted from my third cookbook, Dutch Oven Cooking. *I first developed it when I was teaching a special class where we recreated the lavish barbecue spread from* Gone with the Wind. *It is named after the famed plantation where Scarlett first encounters Rhett Butler.*

MAKES 12 SANDWICHES

1 (4 to 5 pound) bone-in pork picnic shoulder roast

1 tablespoon crushed red pepper flakes

1 tablespoon salt

1 tablespoon black pepper

1 cup apple cider

1 cup apple cider vinegar or white wine vinegar

4 onions, thinly sliced

4 garlic cloves, chopped

1 green bell pepper, seeded and finely chopped

12 large barbecue buns or sourdough rolls

Twelve Oaks Barbecue Sauce (recipe follows)

The night before, rub the outside of the pork shoulder with the red pepper flakes, salt, and black pepper. Place in a zip-top freezer bag and refrigerate overnight.

Remove the pork from the refrigerator and let it sit at room temperature for 1 hour. Preheat the oven to 300° F. Place the pork shoulder in a 5½-quart Dutch oven. Pour the apple cider and the vinegar over and around the pork. Scatter the onions, garlic, and green bell pepper over and around the pork. Cover and roast in the oven for 3½ to 4 hours, or until an instant-read meat thermometer inserted into the pork registers 180° F. Spoon the juices over the pork every 30 minutes during the roasting time. Remove the pork from the pan and let sit for 1 hour before chopping or shredding. Reserve the roasted vegetables and 1 cup of the pan juices.

Chop the pork with a sharp knife or shred the meat by pulling two forks over it. Discard the bone. In a saucepan, combine the chopped pork with the cup of reserved pan juices and all of the vegetables. Stir over medium heat until warm. Ladle hot Twelve Oaks Barbecue Sauce over the pork. Divide among the barbecue buns or sourdough rolls and pass any remaining sauce separately.

TWELVE OAKS BARBECUE SAUCE

MAKES ABOUT 6 CUPS

¼ cup bacon fat or butter, melted

3 onions, thinly sliced

6 garlic cloves, chopped

1 (16 ounce) can chopped tomatoes with their juice

2 cups tomato purée

½ cup Maker's Mark bourbon or any other Kentucky bourbon

¾ cup molasses

½ cup apple cider vinegar

Juice of 3 lemons

¼ cup soy sauce

2 tablespoons Worcestershire sauce

Salt and freshly ground black pepper

⅔ cup assorted chopped fresh herbs, such as mint, lemon balm, rosemary, thyme, and parsley

1 teaspoon Tabasco, or to taste

In a heavy 2½-quart saucepan set over medium heat combine the bacon fat or butter, onions, and garlic. Cook for about 20 minutes, or until the onions are a deep dark brown. Stir the mixture occasionally to prevent the garlic from burning. Stir in the chopped tomatoes, tomato purée, bourbon, molasses, cider vinegar, lemon juice, soy sauce, Worcestershire sauce, and salt and pepper to taste. Simmer, uncovered, stirring occasionally, over low heat for 1 to 1½ hours, or until the sauce is very thick and dark. Stir in the fresh herbs and Tabasco and cook for 15 minutes more. After sauce cools, it can be stored, covered, in the refrigerator for up to 1 month.

Variation: For a Caribbean flair, omit the barbecue sauce and toss the shredded meat with Tropical Fruit Salsa. Serve on split honey-wheat rolls. For a "south of the border" fiesta, omit the barbecue sauce and toss the pork with Tomatillo and Green Chile Salsa. Serve with shredded Monterey Jack cheese and sour cream in warmed flour tortillas.

HEARTY REUBEN LOAF

>⧫>─◦─<⧫<

This is a very unconventional way to serve the classic sandwich reportedly named for its creator, Arthur Reuben (owner of the now-defunct New York City deli of the same name). The original sandwich was supposedly created in 1914 for a lady friend of Charlie Chaplin's and was full of ham (like many of the silent screen stars of the era).

SERVES 6

For the dough:

2½ to 3½ cups bread flour

½ cup whole wheat flour

1 tablespoon caraway seeds

1 package RapidRise yeast

2 tablespoons molasses

1 teaspoon salt

1 cup hot water (120° F)

¼ cup vegetable oil

1 egg, lightly beaten

1 tablespoon yellow cornmeal

For the filling:

1 cup Grainy Homemade Mustard (see page 102)

8 ounces thinly sliced corned beef

⅓ cup Thousand Island dressing

1 cup sauerkraut, rinsed and drained

1 cup grated Swiss cheese

Freshly ground black pepper

For the glaze:

1 egg, beaten with 1 tablespoon water

1 tablespoon sesame seeds

In a food processor combine 2½ cups of the bread flour, the whole wheat flour, caraway seeds, yeast, molasses and salt. Add the water, vegetable oil, and egg to the dry ingredients. Knead, adding enough bread flour in ¼ cup increments to make a soft dough. When the mixture forms a ball in the processor and is no longer sticky, knead about 1 minute longer, until elastic and smooth. Remove the dough and place in a gallon-sized zip-top freezer bag that has been lightly coated inside with nonstick cooking spray. Let rest until doubled, about 30 minutes.

On a lightly floured surface, roll the dough into a 14 x 10-inch rectangle. Carefully place on a baking sheet that has been sprinkled with the cornmeal.

Spread half of the Grainy Homemade Mustard over the dough, coming to within 1 inch of the edges. Layer the corned beef, Thousand Island dressing, sauerkraut, and Swiss cheese lengthwise down the center of the dough. Season to taste with freshly ground black pepper.

To encase the filling, cut the sides of the dough into 1-inch strips down the length of the dough coming to within ¾ inches of the filling. Criss-cross the dough strips: Bring one strip over the center filling and press the end of the strip into the dough on the opposite side.

Next, bring a strip from the other side, also pressing the end into the dough, until the length of the filling is encased with the overlapping strips. Pinch the dough together at both ends and tuck the ends under the loaf. Let rise, uncovered, for about ½ hour.

Preheat the oven to 400° F. Brush the egg glaze on the loaf and sprinkle with the sesame seeds. Bake until golden brown, about 25 to 30 minutes. With 2 spatulas, carefully remove the loaf from the baking sheet and transfer to a wire rack to cool. With a serrated knife cut the loaf into diagonal slices and serve warm or at room temperature, passing the remaining mustard separately.

Variation: Replace the Grainy Homemade Mustard with Mayonnaise with Fresh Herbs, Caper and Green Peppercorn Cream Cheese Spread, or Vidalia Onion Marmalade.

Note: You can freeze several unbaked loaves up to 3 months ahead. See freezing instructions on page 30.

NEW ENGLAND LOBSTER ROLL

>⊱⋯⊱⊶⊙⊷⊰⋯⊰

I first enjoyed this delicious summer sandwich on a weekend trip with friends to Camden, Maine — a surprisingly inexpensive indulgence when purchased from the dockside fishing shacks there. We ate strolling along the pier, seagulls squawking overhead and ready to dive bomb anything we dropped. The lobster was stuffed into soft hot dog buns, but you can use toasted brioche if you prefer.

SERVES 4

4 large soft hot dog buns

1 whole garlic clove, peeled

1½ pounds boiled or steamed lobster meat, coarsely chopped (about 2½ cups)

1 rib of celery, finely chopped

1 cup Dilled Tartar Sauce (see page 115)

2 medium ripe tomatoes, halved and sliced crosswise

16 large fresh basil leaves

Sea salt

Coarsely ground black pepper

1 lemon, cut into 4 wedges

Salt and vinegar potato chips, optional

Crunchy sour pickles, optional

Preheat the broiler. Open the hot dog buns, place face up on a baking sheet, and broil until lightly toasted, about 1 to 2 minutes. Remove from the oven and rub the peeled garlic clove over the toasted buns. Discard the garlic.

In a medium bowl mix together the chopped lobster, celery, and Dilled Tartar Sauce. Line one side of the hot dog buns with tomato slices and the other side with basil leaves. Mound the lobster mixture evenly down the center of the hot dog buns. Season to taste with sea salt and coarsely ground black pepper. Squeeze a wedge of lemon over each open-faced sandwich just before serving. The sandwiches can be made up to 6 hours ahead, tightly wrapped in plastic wrap, and stored in the refrigerator or in an ice chest. Serve with salt and vinegar potato chips and crunchy sour pickles.

Variation: Substitute lump crabmeat (picked over for shells) or boiled and peeled medium shrimp for the lobster and Spicy Cocktail Sauce for the Dilled Tartar Sauce.

MEDITERRANEAN BRAIDED BREAD

I first had this savory "stuffed bread" when I was working with Nathalie Dupree in the late '80s. She had developed a similar recipe and named it for Atlanta Braves baseball hero Dale Murphy. Nathalie swore every time she took this to a home game, the Braves had a victory. I just know every time I serve it, friends always ask for more.

SERVES 6 TO 8

For the dough:
2½ to 3½ cups bread flour
1 package RapidRise yeast
1 tablespoon sugar
1 teaspoon salt
⅔ cup hot water (120° F)
3 tablespoons olive oil
1 egg, beaten
1 tablespoon yellow cornmeal

For the filling:
1 cup Traditional Italian Pesto (see page 112)
¼ cup pitted and sliced kalamata olives
½ cup grated mozzarella cheese
½ cup crumbled feta cheese
½ cup grated Parmesan cheese
6 ounces prosciutto ham
2 roasted red bell peppers (see note on page 117), peeled, seeded and cut into strips
2 tablespoons capers, rinsed and drained

For the glaze:
1 egg, beaten with 1 tablespoon water
2 teaspoons crushed fennel seeds

In a food processor combine 1½ cups of the bread flour, yeast, sugar and salt. Add the water, olive oil, and egg to the dry ingredients. Knead, adding enough flour in ½ cup increments to make a soft dough. When the mixture forms a ball in the processor and is no longer sticky, knead about 1 minute longer, until elastic and smooth. Remove dough and place in a gallon-sized zip-top freezer bag that has been lightly coated inside with nonstick cooking spray. Let rest for 20 minutes.

On a lightly floured surface, roll the dough into a 14 x 10-inch rectangle. Carefully place on a baking sheet that has been sprinkled with the cornmeal.

Spread half of the Traditional Italian Pesto over the dough, coming to within 1 inch of the edges. Layer the olives, mozzarella, feta, and Parmesan cheeses lengthwise down the center of the dough. Place the prosciutto ham, roasted red bell pepper slices, and capers on top of the cheeses. Spread the remaining pesto over the prosciutto layer.

To encase the filling, cut the sides of the dough into 1-inch strips down the length of the dough coming to within ¾ inches of the filling. Criss-cross the dough strips: Bring one strip over the center filling and press the end of the strip into the dough on the opposite side. Next, bring a strip from the other side, also pressing the end into the dough, until the length of the filling is encased with the overlapping strips. Pinch the dough together at both ends and tuck the ends under the loaf. Let rise, uncovered, for about ½ hour.

Preheat the oven to 400° F. Brush the egg glaze on the loaf and sprinkle with the fennel seeds. Bake until golden brown, about 25 to 30 minutes. With 2 spatulas, carefully remove the loaf from the baking sheet and transfer to a wire rack to cool. With a serrated knife cut the loaf into diagonal slices and serve warm or at room temperature.

Variation: Replace the Traditional Italian Pesto with Sun-Dried Tomato Pesto or Green Olive Tapenade, or with half recipes of Mediterranean Artichoke Salsa or Marinated Mushroom Salsa.

Note: Make several of these loaves ahead and freeze on baking sheets immediately after the filling is encased. When the loaves are rock-hard frozen, about 6 hours, remove from the freezer and wrap each individual loaf in plastic wrap and then in heavy-duty aluminum foil. They freeze beautifully in this manner for up to 3 months. To bake, unwrap and place the frozen loaves on cornmeal-coated baking sheets. Lightly cover with tea towels. It will take about 4 to 6 hours for the loaves to defrost and double at room temperature. When ready to bake, remove the tea towels, brush with the egg glaze, sprinkle with the fennel seeds, and proceed as directed above.

CITRUS-GLAZED PORK BUNS

A sandwich buffet is a perfect icebreaker at parties. Guests from varying backgrounds can chat comfortably as they come together to assemble their entrées according to their individual tastes.

Juice and grated zest of 2 lemons

1 cup orange marmalade

2 garlic cloves, chopped

2 tablespoons chopped fresh ginger

½ cup soy sauce

2 tablespoons dark Asian sesame oil

1 teaspoon red pepper flakes

2 tablespoons chopped fresh cilantro

1 (4 pound) boneless pork loin

For serving:

12 to 16 split, soft whole wheat rolls

2 cups baby spinach leaves

2 cups mung bean sprouts, washed and dried

¾ cup Herbed Honey Mustard (see page 117)

Tropical Fruit Salsa (see page 106), optional

In a large bowl combine the lemon juice and zest, orange marmalade, garlic, ginger, soy sauce, dark sesame oil, red pepper flakes, and cilantro. Place the pork loin in a gallon-sized zip-top freezer bag, pour the marinade over the pork, seal the bag, and store in the refrigerator 6 hours or overnight.

Preheat the oven to 400° F. Remove the pork loin from the bag, place it in a shallow baking dish, and surround with the marinade. Place in the center of the oven and roast for about 45 to 50 minutes, or until a meat thermometer registers 145° to 150° F. Transfer the meat to a cutting board and allow to rest 20 minutes before slicing on the diagonal.

When ready to serve, place the sliced pork loin, rolls, baby spinach leaves, fresh bean sprouts, Herbed Honey Mustard, and Tropical Fruit Salsa on the buffet table.

Variation: Serve the sandwiches with Asian Peanut Sauce, Roasted Red Bell Pepper Tapenade, Vidalia Onion Marmalade, Pear and Golden Raisin Chutney, or Fresh Cranberry Orange Relish.

HERB-RUBBED BEEF TENDERLOIN WITH JÍCAMA COLESLAW

I find beef tenderloin quite economical when serving a crowd. This delicious sandwich is ideal for an open house buffet when guests will be arriving at different times.

MAKES 12 TO 16 SANDWICHES

For the coleslaw:

1 large jícama, peeled and cut into 2-inch matchsticks

1 red onion, peeled and thinly sliced

2 carrots, shredded

2 cups sliced radishes

⅔ cup Horseradish and Caper Mayonnaise (see page 106)

2 tablespoons chopped fresh basil

Salt and freshly ground black pepper

For the tenderloin:

2 tablespoons chopped fresh parsley

2 tablespoons chopped fresh rosemary

4 garlic cloves, crushed with 1 teaspoon salt

1 tablespoon black pepper

3 tablespoons coarse-grained Dijon mustard

1 (4 to 5 pound) beef tenderloin, trimmed of all visible fat

12 to 16 split hard rolls

Make the coleslaw: In a large bowl combine the jícama, red onion, carrots, radishes, Horseradish and Caper Mayonnaise, and basil. Season to taste with salt and pepper. Cover and refrigerate for 4 hours or overnight to allow the flavors to mingle.

Make the tenderloin: Preheat the oven to 500° F. In a small bowl combine the parsley, rosemary, garlic crushed with salt, pepper, and Dijon mustard. Rub the herb mixture all over the trimmed tenderloin. Tuck the tail or thinner end of the tenderloin under the rest of the meat so that it will cook more evenly.

Place the meat on the rack of a roasting pan that has been coated with nonstick cooking spray. Place in the center of the oven and roast for 20 minutes. Reduce the heat to 375° F and cook the meat for 20 to 25 minutes, or until a meat thermometer inserted into the thickest part of the tenderloin registers 125° F for rare. (Be sure not to overcook the beef as it will become dry and flavorless.) Remove from the oven and let the meat rest for 20 minutes. Slice very thinly on the diagonal to ensure a delicate texture.

When ready to serve, place the meat on a large platter, the coleslaw in a serving bowl, and the rolls in a napkin-lined basket. Set out additional mayonnaise and Dijon mustard. Allow each guest to assemble his own sandwich, layering the tenderloin and coleslaw on the split rolls.

Variation: If desired, offer an assortment of other toppings, such as Vidalia Onion Marmalade, Mediterranean Artichoke Salsa, Herbed Honey Mustard, Black Olive Tapenade, Caper and Green Peppercorn Cream Cheese Spread, or Gorgonzola Cream Cheese Spread.

RATATOUILLE ON SUN-DRIED TOMATO FOCACCIA

The eggplant, fennel, and black olives impart a Mediterranean flavor to this open-faced "hearth bread." It is perfect served alone or paired with soup or salad. To cut the preparation time, purchase 2 pre-packaged baked thick-crust pizza shells and top with the ratatouille mixture and Parmesan cheese, omitting the first 15 minutes of baking instructions.

MAKES 2 LARGE FLATBREADS

For the dough:

1 package active dry yeast

1 cup warm water (115° F)

1 tablespoon sugar

1 cup Sun-Dried Tomato Pesto (see page 105)

2½ to 3½ cups bread flour

1 teaspoon salt

For the topping:

1/3 cup olive oil

2 Japanese eggplants, thinly sliced

2 red onions, thinly sliced

1 fennel bulb, cored and thinly sliced

1 zucchini, thinly sliced

6 plum tomatoes, thinly sliced

6 garlic cloves, chopped

¾ cup kalamata olives, pitted and halved

¼ cup balsamic vinegar

2 tablespoons chopped fresh rosemary

2 tablespoons chopped fresh basil

Salt and freshly ground black pepper

1½ cups freshly grated Parmesan cheese

Preheat the oven to 400° F. In a 2-cup capacity measuring cup, combine the yeast, water and sugar. Stir to dissolve the yeast. Let the mixture proof for 10 minutes (see note). Add half of the Sun-Dried Tomato Pesto and stir to combine.

In a food processor fitted with the plastic dough blade, combine 2½ cups of the flour and the salt. With the processor running, pour in the yeast mixture slowly until it is absorbed by the flour. Knead until the dough forms a ball and is smooth and elastic, adding more flour in ¼ cup increments as needed.

Lightly grease two baking sheets. Divide the dough in half and roll each half into an oval about 14 x 8 inches. Place the ovals on the baking sheets and press small indentations into the dough with your fingers. Set aside and allow to rise while you make the topping.

In a large deep skillet or sauté pan heat the olive oil over medium-high heat. Add the eggplant, red onions, fennel, zucchini, tomatoes, and garlic. Reduce the heat to medium and cook, stirring occasionally, until vegetables are soft, about 20 minutes. Remove from the heat and add the black olives, balsamic vinegar, rosemary, basil, and salt and pepper to taste.

Divide the mixture evenly among the two ovals. If you

have made your own dough, place in the oven for 15 minutes. Remove from the oven and top with the Parmesan cheese. Return to the oven for 10 to 15 minutes, or until the focaccia is golden brown and crispy around the edges. Move to a rack to cool briefly. Cut into squares or wedges. Serve warm or at room temperature with the remaining Sun-Dried Tomato Pesto. These freeze very well when baked, cooled, and tightly wrapped with heavy-duty aluminum foil. Reheat in the foil at 350° F for about 15 minutes, then unwrap and bake another 5 minutes to re-crisp.

Variation: Vary the flavor of the focaccia by substituting Green Olive Tapenade or Traditional Italian Pesto for the Sun-Dried Tomato Pesto. For a lighter-flavored focaccia, substitute ⅓ cup olive oil for the pesto and replace the ratatouille topping with Mediterranean Artichoke Salsa or Marinated Mushroom Salsa. Bake as directed above, sprinkling Parmesan, Romano, Asiago, or feta cheese over the salsa.

Note: Proofing is actually proving that the yeast is alive and still active. It should become very foamy and bubbly when combined with the warm water and sugar. If it doesn't, start again with a fresh package of yeast. RapidRise yeast does not have to be proofed.

FIESTA CORNMEAL TACO RING

$\rightarrowtail\bullet\circ\bullet\leftarrowtail$

This unique baked bread resembles a beautiful Aztec sun. For serving, hollow out a red bell pepper or fill a small bowl with sour cream. Place in the center of the sandwich ring and garnish with sprigs of fresh cilantro.

SERVES 6 TO 8

For the cornmeal dough:

2½ cups to 3 cups bread flour

½ cup yellow cornmeal, plus additional for dusting the pan

1 package RapidRise yeast

1 tablespoon honey

¾ teaspoon salt

1 cup hot water (120° F)

2 tablespoons vegetable oil

For the filling:

1 pound lean ground beef

3 green onions, chopped

2 garlic cloves, chopped

1 (15½ ounce) can kidney beans, rinsed and drained

1 (8 ounce) can tomato sauce

1 tablespoon chili powder

2 teaspoons ground cumin

Salt and freshly ground black pepper

2 cups Salsa Fresca (see page 113)

1 cup grated cheddar cheese

½ cup grated Monterey Jack cheese with jalapeño peppers

For the glaze:

1 egg, beaten with 1 tablespoon water

Additional cornmeal

Sour cream, for serving

In a large bowl combine 2 cups of the bread flour, the cornmeal, yeast, honey and salt. Stir the water and the vegetable oil into the dry ingredients. Stir in enough of the remaining bread flour to make a stiff dough. Place the dough on a lightly floured surface and knead until smooth and elastic, about 4 to 6 minutes. Cover with a tea towel and let rest on the floured surface for about 10 minutes.

Meanwhile, in a large skillet set over medium-high heat, cook the ground beef, green onions, and garlic for about 5 minutes, or until the meat is browned. Drain and discard any fat from the skillet. Add the kidney beans, tomato sauce, chili powder, and ground cumin. Cook over medium heat, stirring frequently and mashing the beans, for about 10 minutes, or until most of the liquid is absorbed. Season to taste with salt and pepper. Set aside to cool.

Preheat the oven to 400° F. Roll the dough into a 16-inch circle. Place in a greased 14-inch round pizza pan that has been lightly dusted with cornmeal, with the excess dough draping over the edge of the pan. Cut a 7-inch cross in the center of the dough. Cut another X to form 8 even wedges. Spread a 3-inch wide border of the meat/bean mixture evenly around the edge of the dough. Spoon half of the Salsa Fresca over the meat. Sprinkle with the cheddar and Monterey Jack cheeses. Gently pull the cut points from the center of the dough over the filling. Do not stretch the dough as it will tear apart during baking. Press the points into the dough and then fold the overhanging dough over the points. Crimp to seal. Brush with the egg glaze and sprinkle with additional cornmeal.

Place in the center of the oven and bake for 25 to 30 minutes, or until the crust is a nice golden brown. Remove from the oven and transfer to a wire rack to cool. Serve with the remaining Salsa Fresca and sour cream.

Variation: Substitute Tomatillo and Green Chile Salsa or Roasted Red Bell Pepper Tapenade for the Salsa Fresca.

PHILADELPHIA CHEESE STEAK

><∻>∻O∻<∻><

You can make these sandwiches up to one day ahead and refrigerate them. When guests arrive, simply pop the sandwiches into the oven to reheat and melt the cheeses. This hearty steak sandwich is delicious served with golden fried onion rings, potato or macaroni salad made with tangy mustard, and ice-cold beer.

MAKES **2** LARGE FLATBREADS

1 cup Gorgonzola Cream Cheese Spread (see page 111)

6 large hoagie-style rolls, split in half lengthwise

2 cups shredded provolone or mozzarella cheese

3 tablespoons butter

3 tablespoons olive oil

2 garlic cloves, chopped

2 pounds sirloin steak or London broil, very thinly sliced on the diagonal

Salt and freshly ground black pepper

2 sweet onions, such as Vidalia, thinly sliced

1 red bell pepper, seeded and thinly sliced

1 green bell pepper, seeded and thinly sliced

¼ cup chopped fresh parsley

2 tablespoons balsamic vinegar

½ cup freshly grated Parmesan cheese

Preheat the oven to 375° F. Evenly spread the Gorgonzola Cream Cheese Spread on the inside of the hoagie rolls. Sprinkle half of the provolone or mozzarella cheese into the rolls.

In a 12-inch skillet melt the butter and the olive oil over medium-high heat. When the mixture is hot, stir in the garlic and slices of beef. Stir fry for 3 to 4 minutes or until the slices are medium-rare. Remove with a slotted spoon and place in a large bowl. Season to taste with salt and pepper.

Add the onion, red bell pepper, and green bell pepper to the same skillet. Cook over medium heat until crisp-tender, about 2 to 3 minutes. Transfer the contents of the skillet to the bowl with the sautéed steak. Add the parsley and balsamic vinegar. Toss to mix completely.

Divide the meat and vegetable mixture among the 6 prepared hoagie rolls. Top with the remaining provolone or mozzarella cheese and the Parmesan cheese. Wrap each sandwich in aluminum foil and heat in the oven for 8 to 10 minutes, or until the cheese is melted.

Alternately, the sandwiches can be assembled, wrapped in aluminum foil, and refrigerated for up to 1 day. When ready to serve, place the foil-wrapped sandwiches on a baking sheet and place in an oven preheated to 375° F. Heat for 15 to 20 minutes, or until the sandwich is heated through and the cheese is melted. Serve at once.

Variation: Substitute Horseradish and Caper Mayonnaise, Grainy Homemade Mustard, or Caper and Green Peppercorn Cream Cheese Spread for the Gorgonzola Cream Cheese Spread.

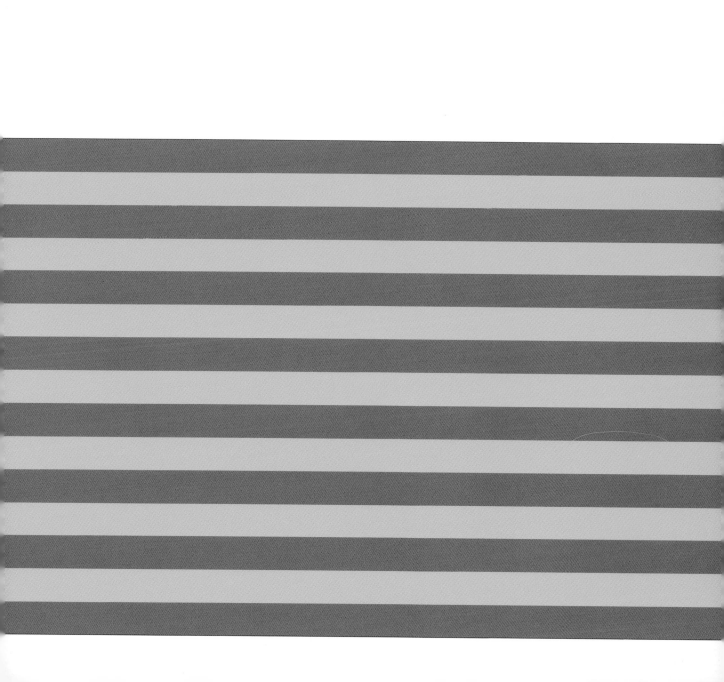

FAST & FLAVORFUL SANDWICHES

Vegetarian Burrito

Roasted Vegetable and Arugula Panini

Western Omelette Roll

Greek Salad Baguettes

Bacon and Veggie Club Sandwich

Tomato, Basil, Fresh Mozzarella, and Prosciutto Panini

Avocado, Sprouts, and Provolone Cheese Melt

Crostini with Anchovies, Olives, and Onions

Lavosh, Turkey, and Hummus Roll

Shrimp and Jícama Crostini

Stilton, Walnut, and Pear on Toasted Brioche

Smoked Trout, Red Onion, and Apple on Rye

Bruschetta Mozzarella

VEGETARIAN BURRITO

For a quick and tasty side dish, mix the remaining Salsa Fresca with 3 cups of hot cooked rice.

SERVES 4

8 (9 or 10 inch) flour tortillas

1 tablespoon peanut oil

1 green bell pepper, seeded and chopped

4 green onions, chopped

2 garlic cloves, chopped

1 zucchini, coarsely chopped

1 (15½ ounce) can pinto beans, rinsed, drained, and lightly mashed

1 (10 ounce) package whole kernel yellow corn, defrosted

2 cups Salsa Fresca (see page 113) or store-bought salsa

1 tablespoon chili powder

2 teaspoons ground cumin

Salt and freshly ground black pepper

1 cup grated cheddar cheese

1 avocado, peeled and sliced

Sour cream

Fresh cilantro

Preheat the oven to 250° F. Wrap the tortillas in aluminum foil and place in the oven to heat.

Coat a large nonstick skillet with nonstick cooking spray and place over medium-high heat. Add the peanut oil and heat until very hot. Reduce the heat to medium and add the green bell pepper, green onions, and garlic. Cook for 5 minutes. Stir in the zucchini, pinto beans, and yellow corn. Cook, stirring occasionally, until the vegetables are tender, about 7 to 8 minutes. Add half of the Salsa Fresca, the chili powder, cumin, and salt and pepper to taste. Simmer, uncovered, for 10 minutes, stirring occasionally, or until the vegetable mixture is thick. Remove from the heat and allow to cool 5 minutes.

To assemble the burritos, remove the warmed tortillas from the oven and unwrap. Spoon the vegetable mixture down the center of each tortilla. Top each with some of the cheddar cheese and a slice of avocado. Roll up and serve with sour cream, fresh cilantro, and the remaining Salsa Fresca.

Variation: Try using Tomatillo and Green Chile Salsa instead of the Salsa Fresca. You can also brush each warmed tortilla with Cilantro and Chipotle Pepper Pesto before filling and rolling, which would be especially good if you are using store-bought salsa.

ROASTED VEGETABLE
& ARUGULA PANINI

This quick supper relies on a store- or bakery-bought focaccia to expedite serving. Panini is the Italian name for roll, or "little breads."

SERVES 4

3 Japanese eggplants, sliced into ½-inch rounds

1 zucchini, sliced into ½-inch rounds

1 yellow squash, sliced into ½-inch rounds

1 red bell pepper, seeded and sliced into rings

1 red onion, thinly sliced

1 cup Garlic Herb Vinaigrette (see page 112)

Salt and freshly ground black pepper

¼ cup balsamic vinegar

½ cup freshly grated Romano cheese

1 large store-bought focaccia (about 10 x 10 inches)

2 bunches arugula

4 ounces shaved fresh Parmesan cheese (see note)

8 large whole basil leaves

Preheat the oven to 450° F. Place the sliced eggplant, zucchini, yellow squash, red bell pepper, and red onion on a large baking sheet. Brush the slices with half of the Garlic Herb Vinaigrette. Season to taste with salt and pepper. Roast the vegetables in the oven for 20 minutes, stirring occasionally. Remove from the oven and toss the roasted vegetables in a large bowl with the balsamic vinegar and Romano cheese.

Cut the focaccia in half horizontally and brush the remaining vinaigrette over the cut sides. Place in the oven directly on the center rack, brushed side up, for about 5 minutes. Remove from the oven, then cut each half into 4 equal squares. Divide the arugula among the 4 bottom squares. Top with the roasted vegetables, shaved Parmesan, and basil leaves. Top with the remaining focaccia squares and press gently. Slice on a diagonal and serve at once.

Variation: Substitute Traditional Italian Pesto or Sun-Dried Tomato Pesto for the Garlic Herb Vinaigrette, or spread the focaccia with Gorgonzola Cream Cheese Spread or Garlic Mayonnaise (Aioli) before warming.

Note: To shave Parmesan cheese, bring the cheese to room temperature, and, with a vegetable peeler, make long even shavings from the block of cheese.

45

WESTERN OMELETTE ROLL

>—+—»—○—«—+—<

This is a perfect fast and flavorful sustenance sandwich for everyone on the go.

1 Kaiser roll, hoagie, or French bread roll

Mayonnaise with Fresh Herbs (see page 104),
   for spreading

1 tablespoon butter

3 large eggs

1 tablespoon heavy cream or milk

1 tablespoon chopped fresh chives

Salt and freshly ground black pepper

½ cup grated cheddar or Swiss cheese (reserve 1
   tablespoon for garnish)

¼ cup finely chopped red onion

¼ cup chopped cooked bacon or ham

¼ cup finely chopped red or green bell pepper

Whole chives, for garnish, optional

Split the bread horizontally and scoop out most of the inner soft bread. Liberally spread inside each half with the Mayonnaise with Fresh Herbs. Set aside.

In an 8-inch nonstick skillet set over medium-high heat, melt the butter. Meanwhile, whisk the eggs, cream or milk, chopped chives, and salt and pepper to taste.

When the butter is hot and lightly browned, add the egg mixture to the skillet. Let the eggs set for 10 seconds, then with a spatula pull the cooked egg from the edges of the pan to the center, allowing the rest of the egg mixture to spread to the edges of the pan. Let the eggs set for another 20 seconds. Pull the eggs to one side of the pan and sprinkle with cheddar or Swiss cheese, red onion, bacon or ham, and red or green bell pepper. Fold the egg in thirds over the filling (like folding a business letter) and cook 15 seconds longer. Gently slide or roll the omelette into the prepared bottom half of the roll. Garnish with the reserved cheese and whole chives, if desired. Cover with the top half and cut in half on a diagonal. Serve at once.

Variation: In place of the Mayonnaise with Fresh Herbs, use Sun-Dried Tomato Pesto, Hot Jalapeño Mustard, Curried Mayonnaise, Caper and Green Peppercorn Cream Cheese Spread, or Green Olive Tapenade.

GREEK SALAD BAGUETTES

For more robust appetites, add strips of marinated grilled lamb, beef, or chicken breasts to the salad mixture.
Steamed or pickled shrimp make a nice addition, too.

SERVES 6

6 small (6-inch) French baguettes

2 cups Hummus Spread (see page 110)

3 cups prewashed spinach leaves, stems removed

1 small red onion, thinly sliced and separated into rings

2 navel oranges, peeled and sectioned

1 (12 ounce) jar marinated artichoke hearts, drained
    and cut in half

2 roasted red bell peppers (see note on page 117),
    seeded and thinly sliced

1 cup pitted kalamata olives

1 cup crumbled feta cheese

1 (2 ounce) can flat anchovy fillets, drained

½ cup whole pepperoncini peppers

Juice of 1 lemon

3 tablespoons extra-virgin olive oil

1 tablespoon chopped fresh oregano

1 tablespoon capers, rinsed and drained

Salt and freshly ground black pepper

Split the baguettes in half horizontally, being careful not to cut through the opposite crust. Remove most of the soft interior bread. With a spoon spread the Hummus Spread inside the baguettes.

In a medium bowl combine the spinach leaves, red onion, orange sections, artichoke hearts, roasted red bell peppers, olives, feta cheese, anchovies, pepperoncini peppers, lemon juice, olive oil, oregano, capers, and salt and pepper to taste.

Divide the salad mixture among the 6 split baguettes and serve at once.

Variation: Traditional Italian Pesto, Horseradish and Caper Mayonnaise, or Green Olive Tapenade makes a wonderful substitute for the Hummus Spread.

BACON & VEGGIE CLUB SANDWICH

>⊷⊶○⊷⊶

My grandmother taught me to sprinkle a pinch of sugar over the bacon as it is frying in the skillet. This adds sweetness as the sugar caramelizes and glazes the crispy strips. For a more robust flavor choose a thick-cut, peppered bacon (sometimes called "country style" bacon). A good store-bought hummus can be substituted for the homemade spread.

MAKES **4** SANDWICHES

12 slices sourdough bread

2 cups Hummus Spread (see page 110)

12 slices bacon

1 carrot, shredded

8 leaves Boston or Bibb lettuce

2 medium tomatoes, thinly sliced

1 small cucumber, peeled and thinly sliced

½ cup crumbled Stilton cheese

1 cup alfalfa sprouts

1 lemon, cut into 4 wedges

Salt and freshly ground black pepper

Carrot sticks, optional

Preheat the oven to 400° F. Place the bread slices on a baking sheet and toast in the oven until golden brown. Spread 1 cup of the Hummus Spread evenly on one side of 8 slices of the bread.

In a large skillet set over medium-high heat, fry the bacon until brown and crisp, turning as needed. Remove and drain on paper towels.

Sprinkle 4 of the bread slices, spread side up, with the shredded carrot, then arrange the bacon on top. Cover the bacon with the lettuce leaves and tomatoes. Top with the 4 plain bread slices.

Next, layer the cucumber slices, Stilton cheese, and alfalfa sprouts. Squeeze a wedge of lemon over each sandwich. Season to taste with salt and freshly ground black pepper. Cover with the remaining 4 slices of toasted bread, spread side down. Press together slightly and then cut each sandwich into 4 quarters. Secure each sandwich quarter with a toothpick. Serve with carrot sticks and the remaining Hummus Spread as a dip.

Variation: Avocado and Yogurt Sauce, Herbed Honey Mustard, Curried Mayonnaise, Garlic Mayonnaise (Aioli), or Horseradish and Caper Mayonnaise makes a nice substitute for the Hummus Spread.

TOMATO, BASIL, FRESH MOZZARELLA, & PROSCIUTTO PANINI

>−◦−<

Like the popular Italian salad, this sandwich's tomato, basil, and fresh mozzarella represent the red, green, and white of the Italian flag. For maximum flavor, be sure the tomatoes are ripe and juicy and the mozzarella is fresh and creamy.

SERVES 6

1 large store-bought focaccia (about 10 x 10 inches)

1 cup Roasted Red Bell Pepper Tapenade (see page 117)

3 green onions, chopped

1 tablespoon capers, rinsed and drained

1 tablespoon chopped fresh oregano

⅓ cup extra-virgin olive oil

¼ cup sherry wine vinegar

Salt and freshly ground black pepper

4 large, very ripe tomatoes, sliced into ¼-inch thick slices

1 pound fresh mozzarella cheese, cut into 24 thin slices (see note)

24 large whole basil leaves

12 ounces thinly sliced prosciutto ham

½ cup freshly grated Parmesan cheese

Basil sprigs for garnish

Cut the focaccia in half horizontally and then into 6 equal squares. Remove the top 6 squares, leaving the focaccia in its original shape. Brush the inner sides of the top 6 squares with the Roasted Red Bell Pepper Tapenade.

In a medium bowl whisk together the green onions, capers, oregano, olive oil, sherry wine vinegar, and salt and pepper to taste. Drizzle evenly over the bottom squares.

Alternately layer the tomato slices, fresh mozzarella slices, whole basil leaves, and prosciutto ham, overlapping on top of the bottom squares of focaccia. Top with the Parmesan cheese. Replace the top squares (those brushed with the tapenade) of the focaccia, then, following the cut marks on the top pieces as a guide, cut through the filling of the sandwich.

Separate into 6 individual servings, slice each on a diagonal if desired, and garnish each with a sprig of fresh basil. Serve at once.

Variation: Substitute Hummus Spread for the Roasted Red Bell Pepper Tapenade.

Note: For the decorative look pictured here, use mozzarella rolled with herbs, roasted bell peppers, or prosciutto.

AVOCADO, SPROUTS, & PROVOLONE CHEESE MELT

The avocado, originally known as "alligator pear," is a luscious fruit known for its buttery texture and mild nut-like taste. To speed up the ripening process, place avocados in a paper bag and leave at room temperature for 3 to 4 days. They should yield to gentle palm pressure when squeezed.

SERVES 4

4 (¾-inch thick) slices ciabatta or other Italian bread

⅔ cup Mayonnaise with Fresh Herbs (see page 104)

4 slices provolone cheese

4 leaves radicchio lettuce

2 plum tomatoes, sliced

1 avocado, peeled and sliced

Salt and freshly ground black pepper

1 cup alfalfa sprouts

Preheat the oven to 400° F. Place the bread slices on a baking sheet and toast in the oven until golden brown.

Remove from the oven and brush each slice with half of the Mayonnaise with Fresh Herbs. Top each piece with a slice of provolone cheese. Return to the oven and bake until the cheese melts, 3 to 5 minutes.

Remove from the oven and arrange the radicchio lettuce, tomato, and avocado over the melted cheese. Season to taste with salt and pepper. Dollop the remaining herbed mayonnaise over the avocado and top with the alfalfa sprouts. Serve at once.

Variation: Try using Garlic Mayonnaise (Aioli), Curried Mayonnaise, Cilantro and Chipotle Pepper Pesto, or Roasted Red Bell Pepper Tapenade in place of the Mayonnaise with Fresh Herbs. For heartier appetites, add thinly sliced turkey, ham, crispy bacon strips, or smoked salmon to the original recipe.

CROSTINI WITH ANCHOVIES, OLIVES, & ONIONS

This hearty and robust open-faced sandwich is not for the faint of heart. The explosion of flavors is phenomenal from first bite to last. It deserves a full-bodied cabernet or merlot to match the strong and assertive flavors of the anchovies, olives, and onions.

SERVES 6

12 (¾-inch thick) slices French bread

1½ cups Vidalia Onion Marmalade (see page 108)

1½ cups grated mozzarella cheese

2 (2 ounce) cans flat anchovy fillets, drained

1 cup pitted kalamata olives

½ cup freshly grated Parmesan cheese

½ cup freshly grated Romano cheese

Preheat the oven to 400° F. Place the bread slices on a baking sheet and divide the Vidalia Onion Marmalade among them. Sprinkle with the mozzarella cheese. Lay 2 or 3 anchovy fillets over the mozzarella on each slice. Sprinkle the olives over the mozzarella and top with the Parmesan and Romano cheeses.

Bake in the oven until lightly browned and the cheese has melted, about 10 to 12 minutes. Remove from the oven and cool for 5 minutes. Serve immediately.

Variation: Replace the Vidalia Onion Marmalade with Sun-Dried Tomato Pesto, Traditional Italian Pesto, or Roasted Red Bell Pepper Tapenade. Sauté 2 sliced onions in 2 tablespoons of butter until soft, about 5 minutes. Place the sautéed onions on top of the pesto or tapenade and proceed with the recipe as described above. For even more flavor, try replacing the anchovies with canned sardines in mustard.

LAVOSH, TURKEY, & HUMMUS ROLL

"Roll-up" sandwiches are more popular now than ever because they are easy to prepare and eat. Soft lavosh, sometimes called Mediterranean flatbread, can now be found at most large grocery stores or specialty bakeries. Pita bread or flour tortillas make an acceptable substitute. For easy party appetizers, cut the rolls into ¼-inch slices and arrange on a round, lettuce-lined platter.

SERVES 8

8 soft lavosh, at least 10 inches in diameter

2 cups Hummus Spread (see page 110),
   or store-bought hummus

1 cup shredded Gruyère cheese

16 ounces thinly sliced turkey breast

2 medium tomatoes, seeded and coarsely chopped

4 green onions, chopped

2 carrots, shredded

1 small cucumber, peeled, seeded, and cut into ½-inch
   dice

½ cup chopped pimento-stuffed green olives

1 cup alfalfa sprouts

Salt and freshly ground black pepper

Spread the hummus on each lavosh leaving a ½-inch border all around. Top with the Gruyère cheese, turkey, tomatoes, green onions, carrots, cucumber, green olives, alfalfa sprouts, and salt and pepper to taste.

Roll up tightly. Cut on the diagonal, seam side down, into 2 halves. Alternately, wrap the whole roll in plastic wrap and refrigerate for up to 1 day. Unwrap and slice just before serving.

Variation: Omit the cucumber in this recipe and substitute Raita Cucumber Sauce, or substitute Avocado and Yogurt Sauce for the Hummus Spread. Have fun experimenting with ingredients — use thinly sliced roast beef and cheddar, honey-cured ham and Swiss, shaved prosciutto and mozzarella, or even smoked chicken and mango chutney.

SHRIMP & JÍCAMA CROSTINI

Crostini literally translated means "little toasts" but there is nothing little about the flavor of this quick entrée. The toast soaks up the flavorful vinaigrette and natural cooking juices, and the jícama offers a sweet crispy-crunch contrast to the savory shrimp. If jícama is unavailable in your area, you may substitute 2 (6 ounce) cans of sliced water chestnuts, drained. For a totally different Asian flavor, try the variation at the end of this recipe.

SERVES 6

12 (¾-inch thick) slices French bread

1 cup Garlic Herb Vinaigrette (see page 112)

4 strips of bacon, coarsely chopped

1 pound large shrimp, peeled and deveined

Salt and freshly ground black pepper

1 small jícama, peeled and cut into 2-inch matchsticks

1 cup quartered cherry tomatoes

1 cup freshly grated Parmesan cheese

2 tablespoons chopped fresh basil

Preheat the oven to 400° F. Place the bread slices on a baking sheet and brush with half of the Garlic Herb Vinaigrette. Bake in the oven until lightly browned. Remove from the oven and set aside.

In a large sauté pan fry the bacon over medium-high heat, stirring occasionally, until golden and crisp, about 5 minutes. With a slotted spoon remove the bacon to paper towels to drain.

Spread the shrimp out on a paper towel and blot dry. Lightly season with salt and pepper. Add the shrimp to the skillet with the bacon drippings and cook over medium heat until they begin to curl and cook through, about 3 to 4 minutes. Remove to a large bowl and add the remaining Garlic Herb Vinaigrette and the jícama. Stir to coat completely.

Place 2 toasted bread slices on each serving plate. Spoon the shrimp and jícama over the toast. Top with the cherry tomatoes, Parmesan cheese, bacon, and basil. Serve at once.

Variation: Omit the Garlic Herb Vinaigrette and substitute Asian Peanut Sauce. Bake the bread slices plain, mixing all of the peanut sauce with the cooked shrimp and jícama. Omit the Parmesan cheese and basil, substituting ½ cup crunchy chow mein noodles, 1 cup pineapple chunks, and chopped fresh cilantro.

STILTON, WALNUTS, & PEARS ON TOASTED BRIOCHE

›—◄•►—◯—◄•►—‹

Brioche is a light yeast bread rich with butter and eggs. Challah would make a wonderful alternative to the brioche, as would a walnut or seven-grain loaf. English Stilton is considered the "king" of the blue cheese family, but any such cheese — a French Roquefort, Danish Saga, Italian Gorgonzola, or Maytag blue — would work equally well.

6 (1-inch thick) slices day-old brioche

1 cup Caper and Green Peppercorn Cream Cheese Spread (see page 111)

12 slices bacon, coarsely chopped

2 ripe Bosc pears, halved, cored, and thinly sliced

1 cup crumbled Stilton blue cheese

Freshly ground black pepper

¾ cup coarsely chopped walnuts

Basil chiffonade for garnish (see note)

Preheat the oven to 400° F. Place the slices of brioche on a baking sheet and toast in the oven for 5 minutes. Remove from the oven and spread each slice with the Caper and Green Peppercorn Cream Cheese Spread.

In a large skillet set over medium-high heat, fry the chopped bacon until golden brown and crisp, about 5 minutes. Remove with a slotted spoon onto paper towels to drain.

Overlap 5 or 6 slices of pear on each slice of bread. Top with the cooked bacon and the Stilton cheese. Season each slice with a generous grinding of black pepper and sprinkle with the chopped walnuts.

Return to the oven and bake until the cheese is melted and the walnuts begin to brown, about 5 minutes. Removed from the oven and sprinkle with the basil chiffonade. Serve hot or at room temperature.

Variation: Substitute Horseradish and Caper Mayonnaise or Vidalia Onion Marmalade for the Caper and Green Peppercorn Cream Cheese Spread.

Note: To make the basil chiffonade, stack 12 to 14 whole large basil leaves, one on top of the other. Roll up the stack of leaves as you would a cigar and then cut the roll on a diagonal into thin strips. Separate the strips.

SMOKED TROUT, RED ONION, & APPLE ON RYE

I enjoy serving this sandwich any time of the year, but it is particularly memorable when cozying up to a crackling fire on a crisp autumn weekend with a chilled glass of Alsatian Riesling. That's my kind of "down time."

SERVES 4

1 Granny Smith apple

1 tablespoon freshly squeezed lemon juice

1 (1 pound) smoked trout, deboned and skin removed

8 slices rye and pumpernickel swirled bread

1 cup Gorgonzola Cream Cheese Spread (see page 111)

1 small red onion, thinly sliced

1 yellow bell pepper, seeded and thinly sliced

Salt and freshly ground black pepper

1 tablespoon capers, rinsed and drained

½ cup chopped pecans, lightly toasted (see note)

2 tablespoons chopped fresh parsley

Halve, core, and thinly slice the apple. Toss with the lemon juice to prevent the slices from turning dark. Pick through the smoked trout for any small bones and flake the fish into bite-sized pieces.

Preheat the oven to 400° F. Place the bread slices on a baking sheet and toast in the oven for 5 minutes. Remove from the oven and spread each slice with half of the Gorgonzola and Cream Cheese Spread. Arrange the apple slices on top of 4 of the bread slices. Top with the smoked trout, onion slices, and yellow bell pepper. Season to taste with salt and pepper. Place a dollop of the cream cheese spread in the center of each sandwich. Sprinkle with the capers, chopped pecans, and parsley, and top with the remaining slices of toasted bread. Serve at once. Plan to use a knife and fork on this one.

Variation: Substitute Grainy Homemade Mustard, Toasted Nut Butter, or Curried Mayonnaise for the Gorgonzola Cream Cheese Spread.

Note: To toast nuts, place them on a baking sheet in a preheated 350° F oven. Toast for 6 to 10 minutes, stirring occasionally, until lightly browned and aromatic. The older the nut is, the more quickly it will toast.

BRUSCHETTA MOZZARELLA

━━◆━◦━◆━━

In Italian bruschetta means "to roast over coals." Traditionally, the split bread is rubbed with a clove of garlic, drizzled with olive oil, seasoned with salt and pepper, and then grilled or broiled. It is delicious, but not even close to being a complete meal. I adapted this creation from a coworker at my first cooking school. More like an open-faced pizza loaf and ready in about 15 minutes, it is a staple in my "good food — fast" department.

SERVES 4

1 loaf Italian bread, cut in half horizontally

1 cup Garlic Herb Vinaigrette (see page 112)

1 teaspoon fennel seeds, crushed

½ teaspoon red pepper flakes

4 green onions, finely chopped

1½ cups quartered cherry tomatoes (about 1 pint)

1 cup pitted green and black olives, sliced

1 cup freshly grated Parmesan cheese

2 cups grated mozzarella cheese

Preheat the oven to 450° F. Lay the bread halves cut side up on a foil-lined baking sheet and brush evenly with the Garlic Herb Vinaigrette. Sprinkle with the crushed fennel seeds and red pepper flakes.

Arrange the green onions, cherry tomatoes, and olives over the bread. Sprinkle the Parmesan and mozzarella cheeses evenly over the bread. Place on the center rack of the oven and bake for 12 to 14 minutes, or until bread is nicely browned and the cheese is melted and bubbly.

Remove from the oven and place on a wire rack to cool for 10 minutes. Slice the bread with a serrated knife into 2-inch pieces, cut on a diagonal if desired.

Variation: Omit all ingredients except for bread and cheeses. Top the split loaf with Mediterranean Artichoke Salsa or Marinated Mushroom Salsa, then sprinkle with cheeses and bake as directed above. For a Southwestern flavor, omit all ingredients except for bread. Top the split loaf with Tomatillo and Green Chile Salsa or Salsa Fresca and sprinkle with 1 cup of shredded cheddar cheese and 2 cups of shredded Monterey Jack cheese with jalapeños. Bake as described above.

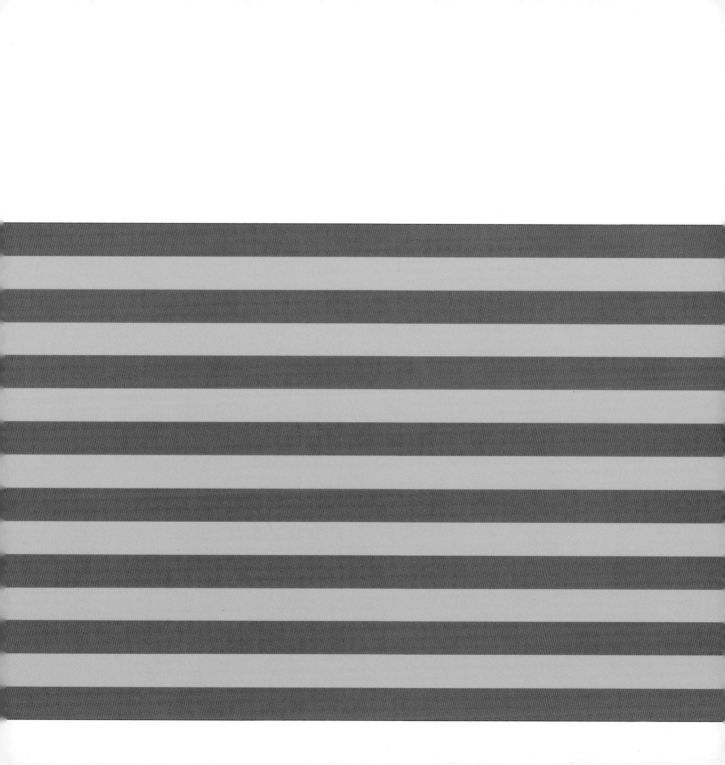

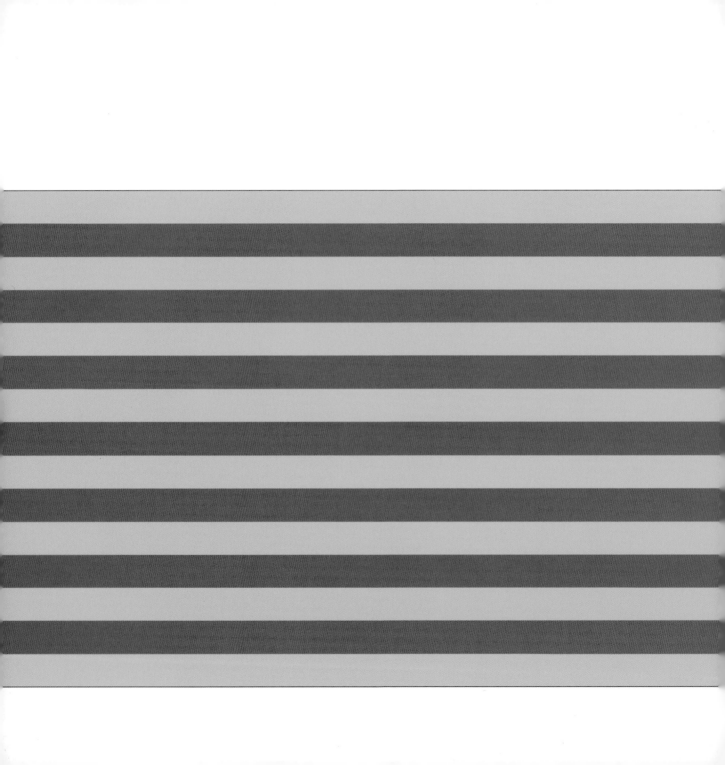

CONTEMPORARY CLASSIC SANDWICHES

Beer-Braised Bratwurst and Sauerkraut Hoagie

Peanut Butter and Banana French Toast

Pan-Seared Salmon "BLT"

Smoked Cheddar Pimiento Cheese Sandwich

Louisville Dungeness Crab Hot Brown

Turkey Sausage, Red Pepper, and Mushroom Sub

Flash-Fried Catfish Nugget Po' Boy

Untidy Josephs

Jamaican Jerked Pork Loin on Toasted Sourdough

Grilled Asparagus Tuna Melt

BEER-BRAISED BRATWURST & SAUERKRAUT HOAGIE

These sausage-filled hoagies, with German potato salad on the side and an assortment of beers, are perfect for fall football parties or an Oktoberfest celebration. Polish kielbasa, Spanish chorizo, or hot Italian sausage makes a great alternate choice for the brats.

SERVES 4

1 tablespoon vegetable oil

2 red onions, thinly sliced

1 red bell pepper, seeded and thinly sliced

1 green bell pepper, seeded and thinly sliced

1 (15½ ounce) can sauerkraut, rinsed and drained

4 large (about 6 to 8 ounces each) fresh German bratwurst sausages

¾ cup Hot Jalapeño Mustard (see page 103)

1 (12 ounce) bottle beer

1 teaspoon caraway seeds

4 hoagie-style rolls, split

1 cup shredded Gruyère cheese

2 tablespoons chopped fresh parsley

Heat the vegetable oil in a 12-inch skillet over medium-high heat. Add the onions, red bell pepper, green bell pepper, and sauerkraut. Cook until the onions are soft, about 8 to 10 minutes.

Prick the sausages all over with a fork and add to the hot skillet with half of the Hot Jalapeño Mustard. Pour the beer into the skillet, then stir in the caraway seeds. Bring to a boil, reduce the heat to low, partially cover, and steam for 20 minutes, or until the sausages are cooked through and no longer pink in the center and the liquid has cooked away.

Brush the inside of the split hoagie rolls with the remaining Hot Jalapeño Mustard. Place a cooked bratwurst in each roll and top with some of the sauerkraut and onion mixture. Sprinkle with the Gruyère cheese and chopped parsley. Serve at once.

Variation: Use Herbed Honey Mustard or Grainy Homemade Mustard in place of the Hot Jalapeño Mustard.

PEANUT BUTTER & BANANA FRENCH TOAST

My nieces, Hope and Emma, love this rendition of Elvis Presley's signature snack. To eat on the run, allow the sandwich to cool about 5 minutes, then wrap in parchment or waxed paper. For Sunday brunch, drizzle the sandwich with warmed maple syrup and serve with seasonal berries and wedges of fresh melon.

MAKES 4 SANDWICHES

3 eggs, lightly beaten

⅓ cup heavy cream or milk

1 teaspoon vanilla

1 teaspoon ground cinnamon

Pinch of salt

8 slices cinnamon raisin bread

1 cup crunchy peanut butter

2 ripe bananas, peeled and sliced

3 tablespoons butter, plus more if needed

Confectioners' sugar, for dusting

In a medium bowl whisk together the eggs, cream or milk, vanilla, cinnamon, and salt.

Spread the peanut butter on one side of each of the cinnamon raisin bread slices. Layer the bananas on 4 slices of bread, then cover with the remaining 4 bread slices. Press the sandwiches gently together to seal.

Lightly coat a large nonstick skillet with nonstick cooking spray, add the butter, and heat over medium heat until the butter is melted. Dip a filled sandwich into the egg mixture, coating both sides. Place in the hot, buttered skillet. Repeat with a second sandwich.

Cook the sandwiches until each side is golden brown, about 1 minute per side.

Add more butter to the skillet if needed and repeat with the remaining 2 sandwiches.

Remove the sandwiches to a plate and slice on the diagonal, or cut into quarters or 4 even strips. Sprinkle with confectioners' sugar and serve at once.

Variation: Substitute Toasted Nut Butter (omitting the Tabasco) for the crunchy peanut butter, or use ¾ cup softened cream cheese mixed with ¼ cup fruit preserves. Sliced peaches, strawberries, or kiwi fruit can be used in place of the bananas.

PAN-SEARED SALMON "BLT"

This is an adaptation of a sandwich served at the Buckhead Diner in Atlanta. I have enjoyed it with pan-seared tuna steaks, shrimp, and scallops, but the most memorable creation had to be for a casual pool party for my best friend Brian's thirtieth birthday. I sautéed lobster tail medallions (fresh off the plane from Inland Seafood), then dipped them in lemon-infused butter. It was without a doubt the best celebration sandwich I have ever served (or eaten).

SERVES 4

8 slices multigrain bread with seeds

8 slices thick-cut pepper bacon

½ teaspoon sugar

4 (6 ounce) salmon fillets

Salt and freshly ground black pepper

1 lemon, cut in 4 wedges

⅔ cup Mayonnaise with Fresh Herbs (see page 104)

8 frisée or curly endive lettuce leaves

24 cherry tomatoes, halved

1 cup chopped broccoli florets or alfalfa sprouts

Preheat the oven to 400° F. Place the bread slices on a baking sheet and toast in the oven for 5 minutes.

In a 10-inch skillet set over medium heat, fry the bacon about 2 minutes, sprinkle with sugar, then continue cooking 6 to 8 minutes, turning once, until browned and crispy. Remove the bacon and let drain on paper towels.

Pat the salmon fillets dry with a paper towel and season each side lightly with salt and pepper. Place the fillets in the same skillet and cook over medium-high heat, about 3 minutes per side, or until the salmon is cooked to medium and the outside of the fish flakes easily with a fork. Squeeze a lemon wedge over each fillet.

Spread the toasted bread slices with the Mayonnaise with Fresh Herbs. On 4 of the bread slices, arrange 2 lettuce leaves, 2 strips of bacon, 1 salmon fillet, 12 cherry tomato halves, and ¼ cup of the broccoli or alfalfa sprouts. Cover with the remaining bread and press gently. Slice the sandwiches in half on the diagonal. Serve at once.

Variation: Try Gorgonzola Cream Cheese Spread, Curried Mayonnaise, or Garlic Mayonnaise (Aioli) in place of the Mayonnaise with Fresh Herbs.

SMOKED CHEDDAR PIMIENTO CHEESE SANDWICH

As a child spending summer vacations on my Granny Lou's farm in North Carolina, I used to crave her "miento cheese." It was a mixture of grated hoop cheese, mayonnaise, and jarred pimientos slathered on store-bought white bread. I have updated this Southern delicacy for the new millennium, making it even better than before. But if memory serves me correctly, it is best enjoyed paired with super-sweet iced tea and eaten while rocking on the creaky front porch swing on a hot summer afternoon.

MAKES 8 OPEN-FACED SANDWICHES

6 strips of bacon, chopped

1 cup grated smoked cheddar cheese

2 cups grated sharp cheddar cheese

½ cup crumbled Stilton cheese

½ cup freshly grated Parmesan cheese

2 ripe Roma tomatoes, seeded and chopped

3 jarred or fresh roasted red bell peppers, chopped (see note on page 117)

4 green onions, chopped

1 teaspoon celery seed

⅔ cup Mayonnaise with Fresh Herbs (see page 104)

¾ cup chopped pecans, lightly toasted (see note on page 58)

Salt and freshly ground black pepper

8 (¾-inch thick) slices ciabatta or other Italian bread

Paprika, for dusting

Preheat the broiler. Lightly coat a large baking sheet with nonstick cooking spray. Set aside.

In a large skillet set over medium-high heat fry the bacon until golden brown and crispy, about 5 minutes. Remove with a slotted spoon to drain on paper towels.

In a medium bowl combine the bacon, smoked cheddar cheese, sharp cheddar cheese, Stilton cheese, Parmesan cheese, tomatoes, roasted red bell peppers, green onions, celery seeds, Mayonnaise with Fresh Herbs, pecans, and salt and pepper to taste.

Divide the mixture among the 8 slices of ciabatta, slightly mounding in the center. Sprinkle with paprika. Place sandwiches on a baking sheet and place under the broiler, about 8 inches from the heat source. Broil until the cheese is lightly browned and bubbly, about 2 to 3 minutes. Serve at once.

Variation: Replace the Mayonnaise with Fresh Herbs with Horseradish and Caper Mayonnaise, Garlic Mayonnaise (Aioli), or Caper and Green Peppercorn Cream Cheese Spread.

Note: This cheese is also wonderful dolloped onto the All-American Sirloin Burger (page 87) or replacing the Gruyère cheese in the Croque Monsieur recipe (page 89).

LOUISVILLE DUNGENESS CRAB HOT BROWN

›‐┼◆►─○─◄┼─‹

The "hot brown," a grilled cheese sandwich combined with a "BLT," was developed at the Brown Hotel in Louisville, Kentucky, in the 1930s. To this day it remains a popular luncheon item in the city. Taking the notion one step further, I added Dungeness crab, the pride of the Pacific coast, making an everyday sandwich something quite extraordinary.

MAKES 4 SANDWICHES

8 strips of thick-cut pepper bacon

Butter, for greasing gratin dishes

4 (¾-inch thick) slices ciabatta or other Italian bread

3 plum tomatoes, cut into thick slices

8 ounces thinly sliced turkey

1 pound pasteurized Dungeness crabmeat, coarsely chopped, or lump crabmeat, picked over for shells

Salt and freshly ground black pepper

2 tablespoons butter

2 tablespoons all-purpose flour

1½ cups milk

1 tablespoon Dijon mustard

1½ cups mixed grated cheddar and Swiss cheeses

Tabasco

2 tablespoons chopped fresh dill

½ cup seasoned bread crumbs

In a large skillet fry the bacon until golden brown. Drain on paper towels.

Preheat the oven to broil. Butter 4 small (2 cup capacity) ovenproof gratin dishes. Lay 1 slice of ciabatta in each gratin. Top with tomato slices, bacon, turkey, and crabmeat. Season to taste with salt and pepper.

To make the sauce, melt the butter in a medium saucepan over medium heat. Add the flour and stir 2 to 3 minutes. Add the milk and stir until the mixture comes to a boil and begins to thicken. Remove from the heat, stir in the mustard and 1 cup of the cheese. Season to taste with salt, pepper, and Tabasco. Pour the sauce over the gratins and sprinkle with chopped dill.

In a small bowl mix together the remaining ½ cup of cheese and the bread crumbs. Sprinkle over the gratins. Place the gratins on a baking sheet and then in the oven about 6 inches from the heat source. Broil until the cheese is melted and bubbly and the top just begins to brown, 1 to 2 minutes. Remove from the oven and serve at once.

Variation: Substitute sautéed shrimp or scallops for the crab. For sheer indulgence, freshly steamed lobster tails, sliced into medallions, would be the way to go.

TURKEY SAUSAGE, RED PEPPER, & MUSHROOM SUB

*Every September I look forward to sampling this classic combo of Italian sausages and peppers
served by New York street vendors in Little Italy. Now you can enjoy it any time of the year.*

SERVES 6

12 small (about 4 ounces each) hot Italian-style turkey
sausages

1 tablespoon vegetable oil

1 red onion, thinly sliced

2 red bell peppers, seeded and thinly sliced

½ cup dry red wine

6 split hero or hoagie rolls

1 cup Grainy Homemade Mustard (see page 102)

2 cups Marinated Mushroom Salsa (see page 115)

1 cup shredded mozzarella cheese

½ cup freshly grated Parmesan cheese

Prick the sausages all over with a fork. Heat the vegetable oil in a 12-inch skillet over medium-high heat. Add the onion, red bell peppers, and sausages and cook for about 10 minutes, or until the sausages are beginning to brown. Add the red wine. Bring to a boil, reduce the heat to low, partially cover, and steam the sausages for 15 minutes, or until the sausages are cooked through and no longer pink in the center and the liquid has cooked away.

Preheat the oven to 400° F. Brush the inside of the hero rolls with half of the Grainy Homemade Mustard. Place 2 cooked turkey sausages into each roll and top with the onion and bell pepper mixture. Top with the Marinated Mushroom Salsa. Sprinkle with the mozzarella and Parmesan cheese. Close the hero tops. Wrap each sub in aluminum foil and place in the oven. Heat for 10 to 12 minutes, or until the cheese is melted and the buns are hot. Remove from the oven. Pass the remaining Grainy Homemade Mustard with the hot subs. Serve at once.

Variation: Use Herbed Honey Mustard or Hot Jalapeño Mustard in place of the Grainy Homemade Mustard and Mediterranean Artichoke Salsa instead of the Marinated Mushroom Salsa.

FLASH-FRIED CATFISH NUGGET PO' BOY

><+>+O+<+><

When I was a child, catfish were often referred to as "bottom feeders" and had a very pronounced flavor. Nowadays, the majority of catfish in fish markets and on restaurant menus is farm-raised. You can substitute tilapia, oysters, shrimp, scallops, or even crayfish tails in this original New Orleans delight. When you are frying the fish, be sure to regulate the heat of the oil. If it is too hot, the catfish will burn and not cook on the inside. If it is not hot enough, the catfish will have a greasy, soggy texture.

SERVES 4

6 catfish fillets, about 6 ounces each

1 cup buttermilk

2 eggs

1 teaspoon Tabasco

1 cup all-purpose flour

1½ cups yellow cornmeal

Salt and freshly ground black pepper

Peanut oil, for frying

2 (14 inch) French baguettes, halved horizontally and then crosswise

1 cup Dilled Tartar Sauce (see page 115)

½ small head iceberg lettuce, shredded (about 2 cups)

1 cup quartered cherry tomatoes

1 small cucumber, peeled, seeded, and cut into ½-inch dice

Dilled pickle slices, for garnish, optional

Rinse and pat the catfish fillets dry with a paper towel. To make nuggets, cut into 1-inch pieces. In a shallow bowl whisk together the buttermilk, eggs, and Tabasco.

In a separate shallow bowl combine the flour, cornmeal, and salt and pepper to taste. Dip a handful of catfish nuggets into the buttermilk, then dredge in the cornmeal mixture. Shake off any excess and place on a wire rack. Repeat with remaining nuggets.

Pour about 3 inches of oil into a large, deep frying pan. Heat to approximately 360° F on a candy thermometer. Fry the nuggets in batches until they are golden brown, 2 to 3 minutes. Remove with a slotted spoon and drain on paper towels. Repeat with remaining nuggets.

Spread the French bread with half of the Dilled Tartar Sauce. Place the lettuce and catfish nuggets on the bottom bread halves. Top with the tomatoes, cucumber, and remaining Dilled Tartar Sauce. Garnish with a few dill pickle slices, if desired, and serve at once.

Variation: Substitute Spicy Cocktail Sauce or Raita Cucumber Sauce (omitting the cucumber in the recipe above) for the Dilled Tartar Sauce.

UNTIDY JOSEPHS

>—+>—◦—<+—<

This is an adult version of that childhood standby known as "loosemeat" in some parts of the country. In the '60s sitcom Family
Affair, *Mr. French, the sophisticated English manservant, suddenly finds himself nanny to three orphaned children.
Always the proper gentleman, French referred to "Sloppy Joes" as "Untidy Josephs"
whenever he prepared Buffy's and Jody's favorite meal.*

SERVES 6

1 red bell pepper, seeded and chopped

1 stalk celery, chopped (about ½ cup)

1 red onion, chopped

1 carrot, shredded

1 pound lean ground sirloin

1 pound ground turkey

3 ounces pepperoni, coarsely chopped

1 cup Spicy Cocktail Sauce (see page 109)

1 (16 ounce) can chopped tomatoes with their juice

1 tablespoon chopped fresh basil

1 tablespoon chopped fresh rosemary

Salt and freshly ground black pepper

6 large sesame seed-topped hamburger buns

1 cup shredded mozzarella cheese

½ cup freshly grated Parmesan cheese

In a 12-inch skillet over medium-high heat combine the red bell pepper, celery, onion, carrot, ground sirloin, and ground turkey. Cook until the meat is browned and the vegetables are soft, 10 to 12 minutes. Drain and discard the excess drippings from the skillet.

Return mixture to the heat and stir in the chopped pepperoni, Spicy Cocktail Sauce, chopped tomatoes, basil, rosemary, and salt and pepper to taste. Simmer, partially covered, over low heat until the sauce is thick and bubbly, about 20 minutes.

Spoon the meat and vegetable mixture evenly over the open buns. Top with the shredded mozzarella and Parmesan cheese. Serve at once while the cheese melts on top.

Variation: Omit the Spicy Cocktail Sauce and use 8 ounces of a commercial spaghetti sauce. If desired, spread the buns with Black Olive Tapenade, Traditional Italian Pesto, Caper and Green Peppercorn Cream Cheese Spread, or Gorgonzola Cream Cheese Spread.

JAMAICAN JERKED PORK LOIN ON TOASTED SOURDOUGH

Do not be intimidated by the list of ingredients for the marinade. You probably have most everything in your pantry right now. Jerk seasoning is a blend of spices that originated in the Caribbean and is used as a dry rub or mixed with liquids to form a marinade. This seasoning combines sweet spices such as cinnamon, cloves, nutmeg, and allspice (sometimes known as Jamaican pepper) with savory flavorings such as thyme, garlic, onion, and dried hot chiles. It can be found in the spice section of most large grocery stores. When a meat is marinated and cooked in this fashion, it is said to be "jerked."

MAKES 8 LARGE SANDWICHES

½ cup apple cider vinegar

3 tablespoons freshly squeezed lime juice

2 tablespoons fresh lime zest

2 tablespoons chopped fresh ginger

¼ cup molasses

4 green onions, chopped

4 garlic cloves, chopped

2 Scotch bonnet, habanero, or jalapeño peppers, seeded and chopped

1 tablespoon jerk seasoning

1 teaspoon allspice

1 teaspoon black pepper

1 (3 pound) boneless pork loin, cut into ¾-inch thick chops

16 slices sourdough bread

16 slices Muenster or Monterey Jack cheese

2 cups tightly packed arugula leaves

2 cups Tropical Fruit Salsa (see page 106)

In a large bowl combine the apple cider vinegar, lime juice, lime zest, ginger, molasses, green onions, garlic, Scotch bonnet peppers, jerk seasoning, allspice, and black pepper. Nestle the pork into the marinade and cover. Refrigerate 6 hours or overnight.

Prepare the charcoal for the grill. When the coals are ash gray (medium-high heat), place the meat on the grill and roast, turning occasionally, until the pork is cooked throughout and the juices run clear when pierced with a fork, about 20 to 25 minutes. Remove the meat to a cutting board and let rest for 10 minutes. With a sharp knife, cut the meat into bite-sized strips.

Place the sourdough bread slices on the grill and toast (or grill) for 3 to 5 minutes, or until lightly browned. Remove and layer 8 slices with the Muenster or Monterey Jack cheese and arugula leaves. Mound the jerked pork over the arugula and top with the Tropical Fruit Salsa. Cover with the remaining 8 bread slices. Serve at once.

Variation: For the Tropical Fruit Salsa, substitute Avocado and Yogurt Sauce or Tomatillo and Green Chile Salsa. Chicken or lamb makes a nice alternative to the pork.

GRILLED ASPARAGUS TUNA MELT

❧

Who says a summer grilling party has to include thick steaks or barbecue ribs? Make fish the light and healthy star of your next cookout. A quick roast over fiery coals and smoked Gouda cheese fully flavor the finished dish. Grilled and butter-basted corn on the cob, drizzled with lime juice and sprinkled with chopped cilantro and sea salt, is my choice for best supporting vegetable.

SERVES 4

1 bunch asparagus

⅓ cup freshly squeezed lime juice

Grated zest of 2 limes

1 cup Garlic Herb Vinaigrette (see page 112)

⅓ cup honey

½ teaspoon red pepper flakes

4 (6 to 8 ounce) tuna steaks, about ¾-inch thick

4 (¾-inch thick) slices sourdough or peasant bread

4 slices smoked Gouda cheese

1 large tomato, thinly sliced

Salt and freshly ground black pepper

4 slices provolone cheese

2 cups Tropical Fruit Salsa (see page 106),
   for serving, optional

Prepare the charcoal for grilling. Blanch the asparagus in boiling water for 1 minute, then drain and refresh under cold running water to stop the cooking. Drain again.

In a medium bowl whisk together the lime juice, lime zest, Garlic Herb Vinaigrette, honey, and red pepper flakes. Place the tuna steaks in a shallow glass dish and pour half of the marinade over the fish. Reserve the remaining marinade. Marinate, uncovered, for 30 minutes, turning the steaks once after 15 minutes. Place the tuna steaks on the hot grill (coals should be ash gray) and discard the marinade in the shallow dish. Cook about 4 minutes per side, turning once. Remove from the grill and place on a platter. Cover with aluminum foil to keep the tuna steaks warm.

With tongs, carefully lay the blanched asparagus on the grill (laying in the opposite direction of the bars). Brush with some of the reserved marinade from the mixing bowl and cook the asparagus until crisp-tender, about 4 minutes. Remove from the grill.

Brush both sides of the bread with some of the marinade from the bowl and place on the grill. Grill for 3 to 5 minutes, or until lightly browned. Turn the bread over. Lay the smoked Gouda cheese on the bread. Top with the grilled asparagus, tomato slices, salt and pepper to taste, and tuna steaks. Brush the steaks with any remaining marinade from the bowl and top with the provolone cheese.

Close the grill and bake just until the cheese melts, about 3 minutes. Carefully remove the crusty open-faced sandwiches with a long spatula and place on individual serving plates. Serve at once with the Tropical Fruit Salsa, if desired.

Variation: Serve this unique sandwich with Pear and Golden Raisin Chutney, Fresh Cranberry Orange Relish, Acar (Spicy Malaysian Pickle Salad), or Mediterranean Artichoke Salsa in place of the Tropical Fruit Salsa.

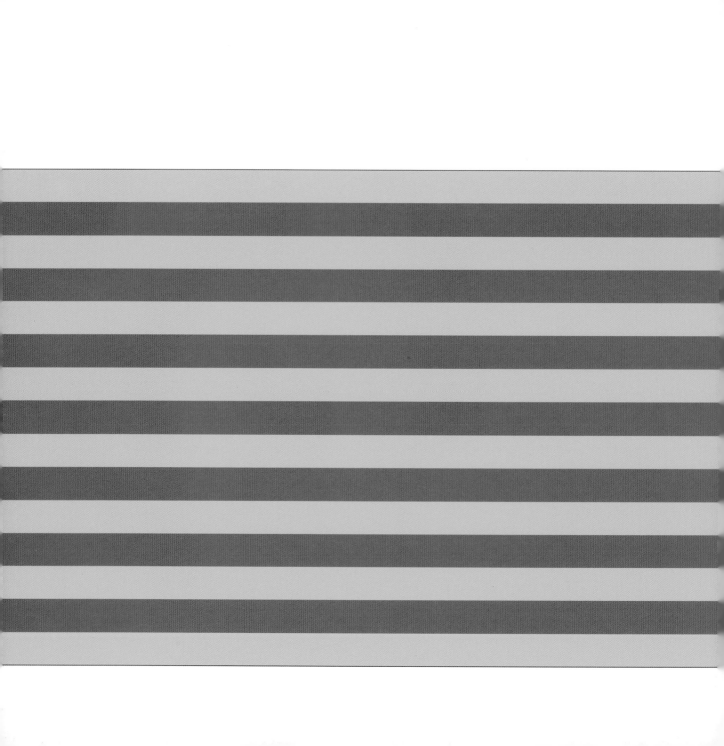

INTERNATIONAL SANDWICHES & BURGERS

All-American Sirloin Burger

Asian Turkey Burger

Grecian Lamb Burger

Cuban Pork and Black Bean Burger

Croque Monsieur with Sliced Tomato

Italian Portobello Mushroom and Goat Cheese Sandwich

Chili-Rubbed Turkey Fajitas

Baby Shrimp Quesadillas

Asian Duck Salad Sandwich

Tandoori-Style Chicken Breast with Pears and Golden Raisins

ALL-AMERICAN SIRLOIN BURGER

>—⊷—○—⊷—<

Now an American icon, the hamburger is believed to have made its debut in the States at the St. Louis/Louisiana Purchase Exposition in 1904. The name "hamburger" comes from the seaport town of Hamburg, Germany, where an ingenious chef decided to cook the raw shredded beef (today known as steak tartare) brought by sailors from the Baltic provinces of Russia. A few tips to ensure a juicy burger: Use the best quality beef available, add ice water for moistness, handle the meat as little as possible, and do not overcook the patties.

SERVES 4

2 pounds lean ground sirloin

1 egg, lightly beaten

⅓ cup ice-cold water

Salt and freshly ground black pepper

4 large onion rolls or hamburger buns

4 slices cheddar cheese, optional

Mayonnaise and mustard

4 whole red oak lettuce leaves

1 Vidalia onion, thinly sliced

1 large tomato, thinly sliced

Dill pickle slices

Ketchup

In a large bowl combine the ground sirloin, egg, water, and salt and pepper to taste. Form into 4 patties about 1-inch thick. Place on a platter and cover with plastic wrap. Refrigerate until you are ready to grill, up to 24 hours.

Prepare the charcoal for the grill. When the coals are ash gray (medium-high heat), place the buns on the grill, cut side down, and toast until lightly browned, about 2 minutes. Remove to a serving platter.

Place the patties on the grill rack and cook 3 to 4 minutes on one side. Turn and grill on the second side, 5 to 6 minutes for medium-rare. Top with the cheddar cheese, if desired, and grill for 1 more minute, or until the cheese begins to melt.

Spread mayonnaise on half of each onion roll or hamburger bun and mustard on the other half. Place the lettuce leaves and slices of onion on the bottom of the rolls. Place the grilled patties on top of the onion. Top with the tomato slices and dill pickles. Season once more with salt and pepper to taste. Drizzle with ketchup and place the other half of the bun on top. Press gently together and serve at once.

Note: The burgers can also be pan-fried in a skillet with 1 tablespoon of vegetable oil. Cook over medium-high heat 4 minutes on one side and 5 to 6 minutes on the other. Also, they can be broiled in the oven about 6 inches from the heat source for the same length of time as for grilling.

Variation: Experiment with Vidalia Onion Marmalade, Avocado and Yogurt Sauce, Mediterranean Artichoke Salsa, Sun-Dried Tomato Pesto, or Gorgonzola Cream Cheese Spread. Use different cheeses, such as Gruyère, mozzarella, blue, Monterey Jack with peppers, or Havarti — whatever suits your tastes. Top with crispy bacon, Canadian bacon, sautéed mushrooms, or stir-fried red and green bell pepper strips.

ASIAN TURKEY BURGER

—◆—○—◆—

East meets west in this unique offering of Yankee ingenuity. You can also shape the ground turkey into oblong ovals, grill as directed below, wrap the cooked burger in large warmed Chinese pancakes or flour tortillas, and garnish with the topping of your choice.

SERVES 4

2 pounds lean ground turkey

⅓ cup applesauce

¼ cup Hoisin sauce

1 tablespoon soy sauce

1 tablespoon dark Asian sesame oil

1 tablespoon chopped fresh ginger

2 garlic cloves, chopped

3 green onions, chopped

Salt and freshly ground black pepper

4 sesame seed-topped hamburger buns

4 Napa cabbage leaves

1 (6 ounce) can sliced water chestnuts, drained

¼ pound mung bean sprouts, washed and dried

4 green onions, slivered on a diagonal

⅔ cup Asian Peanut Sauce (see page 103)

In a large bowl combine the ground turkey, applesauce, Hoisin sauce, soy sauce, dark Asian sesame oil, ginger, garlic, green onions, and salt and pepper to taste. Form into 4 patties about 1-inch thick. Place on a platter and cover with plastic wrap. Refrigerate until you are ready to grill, up to 24 hours.

Prepare the charcoal for the grill. When the coals are ash gray (medium-high heat), place the buns on the grill, cut side down, and toast until lightly browned, about 2 minutes. Remove to a serving platter.

Place the patties on the grill rack and cook about 6 to 7 minutes on one side. Turn and grill on the second side, about 8 to 10 minutes, making sure the turkey is no longer pink in the center and the juices run clear when pierced with a fork.

Place the Napa cabbage leaves on the bottoms of the buns. Lay the grilled patties on top. Top the patties with the water chestnuts, bean sprouts, and slivered green onions. Season once more with salt and pepper to taste. Drizzle with the Asian Peanut Sauce. Cover with the other halves of the buns. Press gently together and serve at once.

83

Note: The burgers can also be pan-fried in a skillet with 1 tablespoon of vegetable oil. Cook over medium heat 6 minutes on one side and about 10 to 12 on the other. Also, they can be broiled in the oven about 6 inches from the heat source for the same length of time as for grilling.

Variation: As an alternative to the Asian Peanut Sauce, top the burger with Hot Jalapeño Mustard, Cilantro and Chipotle Pepper Pesto, Curried Mayonnaise, Pear and Golden Raisin Chutney, Raita Cucumber Sauce, or Acar (Spicy Malaysian Pickle Salad).

GRECIAN LAMB BURGER

To keep a Greek theme, serve these burgers alongside tabbouleh (bulgur wheat and parsley salad) and dolmades (stuffed grape leaves) or a fresh vegetable platter with Hummus Spread (see page 110) as a dip. To save time for a midsummer night's al fresco feast, contact a Middle Eastern deli in your area and have them prepare the side dishes. And you might as well pick up the baklava for dessert while you're there!

SERVES 4

1½ pounds lean ground lamb

2 garlic cloves, chopped

3 green onions, chopped

1 (10 ounce) package frozen chopped spinach, defrosted and squeezed dry

1 egg, lightly beaten

⅓ cup seasoned bread crumbs

1 tablespoon chopped fresh mint

1 tablespoon chopped fresh oregano

1 tablespoon chopped fresh rosemary

2 teaspoons ground cumin

1 teaspoon fennel seed, crushed

½ teaspoon cayenne pepper

Salt and freshly ground black pepper

4 whole-wheat pitas, cut in half to make 8 pockets

2 cups Raita Cucumber Sauce (see page 107)

12 frisée lettuce leaves

1 cup cherry tomato halves

1 cup crumbled feta cheese

1 cup kalamata olives, pitted and sliced

In a large bowl combine the ground lamb, garlic, green onions, spinach, egg, bread crumbs, mint, oregano, rosemary, cumin, fennel seed, cayenne pepper, and salt and pepper to taste. Form into 4 patties about 1-inch thick. Place on a platter and cover with plastic wrap. Refrigerate until you are ready to grill, up to 24 hours.

Prepare the charcoal for the grill. When the coals are ash gray (medium-high heat), place the pita halves on the grill and toast until lightly browned, about 1 to 2 minutes per side. Remove to a serving platter.

Place the patties on the grill and cook about 5 to 6 minutes on one side. Turn and grill on the second side, about 6 to 8 minutes, making sure the lamb is just slightly pink in the center. Remove to a clean platter and let rest for about 5 minutes.

Drizzle some of the Raita Cucumber Sauce in each of the pita pockets. Cut the lamb patties in half and slide one into each pocket. Place the frisée and cherry tomatoes on each side of the lamb. Drizzle with more of the Raita Cucumber Sauce and then top each pita with feta cheese and black olives. Serve at once.

Note: The burgers can also be pan-fried in a skillet with 1 tablespoon of vegetable oil. Cook over medium heat 8

minutes on one side and about 6 to 8 minutes on the other. Also, they can be broiled in the oven about 6 inches from the heat source for the same length of time as for grilling.

Variation: Instead of the Raita Cucumber Sauce, top the Grecian Lamb Burgers with Mediterranean Artichoke Salsa, Marinated Mushroom Salsa, Garlic Herb Vinaigrette, Avocado and Yogurt Sauce, Hummus Spread, Green Olive Tapenade, or Black Olive Tapenade.

CUBAN PORK
& BLACK BEAN BURGER

>⊢→◆→○←◆⊣<

*I first created this dish on a week-long hiatus in Bermuda. Having gone to the market earlier in the day, then lounged on the beach
with more than one Mojita (an iced concoction of white rum, mint sugar syrup, freshly squeezed lime juice, and
club soda), we were famished by dinnertime. These savory burgers served with deep-fried slices
of plantains made the evening festivities with close friends even more memorable.*

SERVES 4

1 pound lean ground pork

½ pound lean ground veal or turkey

1 (15½ ounce) can black beans, drained and rinsed

2 garlic cloves, chopped

3 green onions, chopped

1 egg, lightly beaten

⅓ cup seasoned bread crumbs

1 tablespoon chili powder

2 teaspoons ground cumin

½ teaspoon cayenne pepper

Salt and freshly ground black pepper

4 ciabatta rolls, or other Italian rolls, cut in half
horizontally

1 cup Cilantro and Chipotle Pepper Pesto (see page 105)

4 slices smoked Gouda cheese

4 Romaine lettuce leaves

4 (⅓-inch thick) pineapple slices, peeled and cored

1 avocado, peeled and sliced

In a large bowl combine the ground pork, ground veal or turkey, black beans, garlic, green onions, egg, bread crumbs, chili powder, ground cumin, cayenne pepper, and salt and pepper to taste. Form into 4 patties about 1-inch thick. Place on a platter and cover with plastic wrap. Refrigerate until you are ready to grill, up to 24 hours.

Prepare the charcoal for the grill. When the coals are ash gray (medium-high heat), place the halved rolls on the grill, cut side down, and toast until lightly browned, about 2 minutes. Remove to a serving platter.

Place the patties on the grill and cook about 6 to 8 minutes on one side. Turn and grill on the second side, about 8 to 10 minutes, making sure the pork is cooked throughout and the juices run clear when pierced with a fork. Remove to a clean platter and let rest for about 10 minutes.

Brush the Cilantro and Chipotle Pepper Pesto on the bottom half of each roll. Top with the burger, smoked Gouda cheese, Romaine lettuce leaves, pineapple, and avocado slices. Season once more with salt and pepper to taste. Drizzle with the remaining Cilantro and Chipotle Pepper Pesto and cover with the top half of the roll. Press gently together and serve at once.

Note: The burgers can also be pan-fried in a skillet with 1 tablespoon of vegetable oil. Cook over medium heat 8 minutes on one side and about 8 to 9 minutes on the other. Also, they can be broiled in the oven about 6 inches from the heat source for the same length of time as for grilling.

Variation: Instead of the Cilantro and Chipotle Pepper Pesto, try Tropical Fruit Salsa, Tomatillo and Green Chile Salsa, Vidalia Onion Marmalade, Avocado and Yogurt Sauce, or Pear and Golden Raisin Chutney.

CROQUE MONSIEUR
WITH SLICED TOMATO

This classic French bistro sandwich has to be one of my favorite noonday meals, especially when served with potato salad or coleslaw and tiny French cornichons or pickled okra. For a delicious Sunday brunch, top the pan-fried sandwiches with butter-sautéed spinach and poached eggs, then drizzle with Hollandaise sauce. For a Monte Cristo sandwich, substitute thinly sliced roast chicken for the ham and Swiss cheese for the Gruyère.

MAKES 4 SANDWICHES

3 eggs, lightly beaten

⅓ cup heavy cream or milk

½ teaspoon salt

Pinch of cayenne pepper

⅔ cup Mayonnaise with Fresh Herbs (see page 104)

8 slices white bread

4 slices Gruyère cheese

4 slices honey-cured ham

1 large vine-ripe tomato, sliced

Salt and freshly ground black pepper

4 tablespoons butter

2 tablespoons olive oil

In a medium bowl whisk together the eggs, cream or milk, salt, and cayenne pepper.

Spread the Mayonnaise with Fresh Herbs over one side of each slice of bread. Place a slice of Gruyère on 4 of the slices, followed by the ham, tomato slices, and salt and pepper to taste. Top each sandwich with a second slice of bread, pressing down firmly.

Lightly spray a large nonstick skillet with nonstick cooking spray, add 2 tablespoons of the butter and the olive oil, and heat over medium heat until the butter is melted and hot. Dip 2 sandwiches into the egg mixture, coating on both sides. Place in the hot, buttered skillet and cook the sandwiches over medium heat until each side is golden brown and the cheese has melted, 1 to 2 minutes per side.

Add the remaining 2 tablespoons of butter to the skillet. When it is melted and hot, dip the other two sandwiches in the egg mixture, then cook them until golden brown. Cut each sandwich into 4 quarters and serve immediately.

Variation: Substitute Herbed Honey Mustard, Horseradish and Caper Mayonnaise, Garlic Mayonnaise (Aioli), or Gorgonzola Cream Cheese Spread for the Mayonnaise with Fresh Herbs.

ITALIAN PORTOBELLO MUSHROOM & GOAT CHEESE SANDWICH

Portobello mushrooms are not Italian in origin. The romantic-sounding name was conceived by some industrious farmers in the early '80s to help these larger versions of the common brown mushroom sell better. Because the portobello is left to fully mature, it develops a heartier flavor and chewier texture perfect for roasting or grilling whole. You may sometimes see this mushroom spelled with an A. Both portobello and portobella are considered acceptable spellings.

SERVES 4

4 large portobello mushroom caps, stems discarded

2 red bell peppers, halved and seeded

1 red onion, thinly sliced

1 cup Garlic Herb Vinaigrette (see page 112)

6 ounces soft goat cheese such as Montrachet or chèvre

1 large focaccia (about 10 x 10 inches)

1 head radicchio lettuce, thinly sliced

1 fennel bulb, cored and thinly sliced (chop and reserve the fronds for garnish)

12 large whole basil leaves

½ cup pitted kalamata olives

½ cup freshly grated Parmesan cheese

Salt and freshly ground black pepper

Preheat the oven to 400° F. Place the mushrooms, stem side down, red bell pepper halves, and red onion slices on a foil-lined baking sheet. Brush the vegetables with half of the Garlic Herb Vinaigrette. Roast in the oven for 15 minutes. Remove from the oven, turn the mushrooms over and fill the caps with the goat cheese. Return vegetables to the oven and bake for 5 minutes, or until the cheese melts. Remove from the oven. Let cool 10 minutes, then slice the mushrooms and red bell pepper into strips.

Cut the focaccia into 4 quarters, then cut each quarter in half horizontally. Brush the cut sides of each quarter with the remaining Garlic Herb Vinaigrette. Place in the oven directly on the center rack and bake, cut side up, for 5 to 7 minutes, or until lightly toasted.

Remove the focaccia from the oven. Top the bottom 4 slices of toasted focaccia with the radicchio and fennel. Next, layer with the mushroom and red bell pepper strips, onion slices, and basil leaves. Scatter the black olives and Parmesan cheese over the basil, season well with salt and pepper, and garnish with the chopped fennel fronds. Top with the remaining focaccia halves and serve at once.

Variation: For a deep, smoky flavor, grill the vegetables instead of roasting. Grill over medium-hot coals, mushrooms stem side down, for 3 minutes. Turn all the vegetables and fill the mushroom caps with the cheese. Close the grill lid and continue cooking about 5 minutes, or until the cheese has melted. Remove the vegetables from the grill. Grill the focaccia, cut side down, for about 2 minutes, then proceed as directed above. In addition to the Garlic Herb Vinaigrette, you can spread the toasted focaccia slices with Green Olive Tapenade, Sun-Dried Tomato Pesto, Gorgonzola Cream Cheese Spread, or Garlic Mayonnaise (Aioli).

CHILI-RUBBED TURKEY FAJITAS

><+>-0-<+><

Fat-free flour tortillas, nonfat sour cream, and reduced-fat cheddar cheese transform this already low-fat recipe into an even more heart-healthy entrée. Pay close attention to the spices in the ingredients list. Chili powder is a seasoning blend of dried chiles, garlic, onion, oregano, cumin, coriander, salt, and pepper — not to be mistaken for "pure ground chiles," which are equivalent to red pepper (or cayenne) in heat and would be unmercifully fiery in this quantity if accidentally substituted.

SERVES 8

16 (8 inch) flour tortillas

2 pounds lean turkey breast cutlets

2 tablespoons chili powder

2 teaspoons ground cumin

½ teaspoon cayenne pepper

1 tablespoon canola oil

1 red bell pepper, seeded and thinly sliced

1 green bell pepper, seeded and thinly sliced

2 red onions, thinly sliced

3 garlic cloves, thinly sliced

Juice of 2 limes

2 tablespoons chopped fresh oregano

Salt and freshly ground black pepper

Garnishes:

Shredded iceberg lettuce

Chopped tomatoes

Sour cream

Grated cheddar cheese

2 cups Tropical Fruit Salsa (see page 106)

Preheat the oven to 425° F. Wrap the tortillas in aluminum foil and set aside. Pound the turkey breast cutlets between two pieces of plastic wrap until very thin. On a piece of waxed paper, mix together the chili powder, cumin, and cayenne. Rub this mixture into the turkey cutlets with your fingers. Place on a baking sheet that has been lightly coated with nonstick cooking spray. Place in the oven and cook about 6 to 8 minutes per side, turning once. Remove and slice the roasted turkey into thin strips. Reduce the oven temperature to 250° F and place the wrapped tortillas in the oven to heat.

In a 12-inch skillet heat the oil over medium-high heat. Add the red bell pepper, green bell pepper, red onions, and garlic. Cook until the peppers are softened and the onions begin to wilt, about 5 minutes. Stir in the lime juice, oregano, and salt and pepper to taste.

Add the turkey strips and toss over medium heat for 1 minute. Transfer the mixture to a large serving platter, and let each person assemble his own fajita.

Variation: Try Tomatillo and Green Chile Salsa, Salsa Fresca, Avocado and Yogurt Sauce, or Cilantro and Chipotle Pepper Pesto as garnishes.

BABY SHRIMP QUESADILLAS

<hr>

For a vegetarian alternative, substitute 1 cup of jícama, cut into matchsticks, for the shrimp. For a bit of variety, try adding smoked chicken, crabmeat, or thinly sliced roast beef or lamb to the filling mixture. These quesadillas can be made ahead, stacked between layers of plastic wrap, then wrapped in aluminum foil and refrigerated for up to 24 hours.

SERVES 6

⅓ cup sour cream

1 (3 ounce) package cream cheese, softened

4 green onions, chopped

2 teaspoons chili powder

1 teaspoon ground cumin

1 (4 ounce) can sliced black olives, drained

1 pound cooked baby shrimp, peeled

1 cup grated sharp cheddar cheese

1 cup grated Monterey Jack cheese

Salt and freshly ground black pepper

24 (8 inch) flour tortillas

1 cup Cilantro and Chipotle Pepper Pesto
(see page 105)

1 egg white, beaten until frothy

Peanut or vegetable oil

Salsa Fresca (see page 113) and additional sour
cream

In a large bowl combine the sour cream, cream cheese, green onions, chili powder, cumin, black olives, baby shrimp, cheddar cheese, Monterey Jack cheese, and salt and pepper to taste.

Place ¼ cup of the mixture on a tortilla and spread to ½ inch of the edge. Drizzle with the Cilantro and Chipotle Pepper Pesto. Brush the edge of the tortilla with the beaten egg white and place a second tortilla on top, pressing to seal the edges. Repeat with the remaining tortillas.

Lightly brush a 12-inch nonstick skillet or well-seasoned cast iron griddle with the oil. Heat over medium-high heat until sizzling hot. Reduce the heat to medium and quickly cook the tortillas, turning once, 1 to 2 minutes per side. Remove from the pan and place on paper towels. Let the quesadillas rest for about 5 minutes to allow the cheeses to set. Cut each quesadilla into 6 wedges. Serve with Salsa Fresca and additional sour cream.

Variation: For an exotic flair, substitute Asian Peanut Sauce for the Cilantro and Chipotle Pepper Pesto and serve with Acar (Spicy Malaysian Pickle Salad) in place of the Salsa Fresca.

These quesadillas are also delicious served with Spicy Cocktail Sauce, Tropical Fruit Salsa, or Tomatillo and Green Chile Salsa.

ASIAN DUCK SALAD SANDWICH

>–+–◆>–+–◯–+–<◆–+–<

The succulence of the duck breast in this elegant wrapped sandwich is enhanced by a flavorful sauce and contrasting texture from the crunchy vegetables. As an alternative to broiling the duck breasts, you can grill them, skin side down, over medium-hot coals, or pan-fry them in 2 tablespoons each of butter and olive oil over medium-high heat. Do not cook the duck breasts for more than 10 minutes, as they will become very dry and tough. Chicken makes a worthy substitute for the duck, although not quite as rich — just make sure to broil the chicken until the juices run clear, about 20 minutes (turning once after 10 minutes).

SERVES 6

6 boned duck breasts with skin, about 6 ounces each

Salt and freshly ground black pepper

½ cup Hoisin sauce

½ head radicchio lettuce, very thinly sliced

1 carrot, shredded

4 green onions, slivered on a diagonal

1 cup mung bean sprouts, washed and dried

1 (6 ounce) can sliced water chestnuts, drained

⅓ cup golden raisins

⅔ cup Asian Peanut Sauce (see page 103)

6 large (10 inch) flour tortillas

½ cup fresh raspberries or dried cherries

½ cup unsalted cashews, lightly toasted (see note on page 58)

Preheat the broiler for 15 minutes. Season the duck breasts with salt and pepper to taste. Place on a broiler rack and broil about 6 inches from the heat source about 9 to 10 minutes, turning once, until medium rare. Turn off the oven and remove the duck breasts to a cutting board, brush with the Hoisin sauce, and cover with aluminum foil to keep warm. Wrap the flour tortillas in aluminum foil and place in the oven. The residual heat from the broiler will warm the tortillas in about 7 or 8 minutes. When ready to serve, cut each duck breast crosswise on a diagonal into thin strips.

In a large bowl toss together the radicchio, carrot, green onions, bean sprouts, water chestnuts, and golden raisins with half of the Asian Peanut Sauce. Divide this mixture among the warmed flour tortillas. Top with the sliced duck breast, then drizzle with the remaining Asian Peanut Sauce. Top with the fresh raspberries or dried cherries and toasted cashews. Wrap the tortillas around the filling and serve at once.

Variation: Omit the Asian Peanut Sauce and spread the warmed tortillas (and later, top the sliced duck breast) with Toasted Nut Butter, Hot Jalapeño Mustard, or Herbed Honey Mustard, then toss the vegetables with Curried Mayonnaise.

TANDOORI-STYLE CHICKEN BREAST WITH PEARS AND GOLDEN RAISINS

><+>+0+<+><

This easy marinade helps the home cook achieve a taste very similar to that of meats cooked in an Indian tandoor oven — a tall, cylindrical clay oven capable of producing intense, smoky heat, thus sealing in moistness and flavor. You can substitute pork loin or lamb for the chicken with equally incredible results.

6 (8 inch) green onion tops

1 teaspoon ground cumin

1 teaspoon ground coriander

1 teaspoon ground ginger

1 teaspoon ground cardamom

1 teaspoon cayenne pepper

1 teaspoon salt

1 teaspoon black pepper

½ teaspoon ground turmeric

1 small onion, peeled and cut into quarters

2 garlic cloves, peeled

1 jalapeño or serrano pepper, seeded and chopped

1 tablespoon chopped fresh ginger

1 cup plain low-fat yogurt

6 boneless, skinless chicken breasts

1 cup thinly sliced Romaine lettuce

2 carrots, shredded

1 cup mung bean sprouts, washed and dried

2 cups Raita Cucumber Sauce (see page 107)

6 large, soft lavosh or flatbreads

2 cups Pear and Golden Raisin Chutney (see page 107)

Blanch the green onion tops in boiling salted water for about 1 minute or until pliable. Drain and reserve.

In a small skillet set over medium heat combine the cumin, coriander, ginger, cardamom, cayenne pepper, salt, pepper, and turmeric. Stir constantly until mixture just begins to smoke. Remove from the heat and set aside.

In a food processor combine the onion, garlic, jalapeño or serrano pepper, and ginger. Pulse until finely chopped. Add the toasted spices and the yogurt. Process until smooth. Place the chicken in a baking dish and top with the yogurt marinade. Cover and marinate, refrigerated, at least 2 hours or up to 24 hours.

Preheat the broiler for 15 minutes. Place the chicken on a broiler rack and cook, about 8 inches from the heat source, for 15 minutes, turning once after 7 to 8 minutes. Remove to a cutting board and allow to rest for 10 minutes. Cut the chicken into slices on a diagonal.

In a large bowl toss together the sliced Romaine, carrots, bean sprouts, and half of the Raita Cucumber Sauce. Divide the vegetables among the lavosh or flatbreads, and top each with the sliced Tandoori chicken. Spoon more of the Raita Cucumber Sauce over the chicken and dollop some of the Pear and Golden Raisin Chutney on top. Roll up one end of the flatbread or lavosh like a horn and tie the end with a green onion top to secure. Repeat with remaining flatbreads and serve at once, passing any remaining chutney separately.

Variation: For the Pear and Golden Raisin Chutney, you can substitute 1 cup of store-bought mango chutney (such as Major Grey's), ½ cup golden raisins, and ½ cup chopped, toasted almonds, pecans, or walnuts. The filling is also delicious wrapped in warmed flour tortillas. The vegetables in the recipe can be tossed with Curried Mayonnaise or Avocado and Yogurt Sauce instead of Raita Cucumber Sauce.

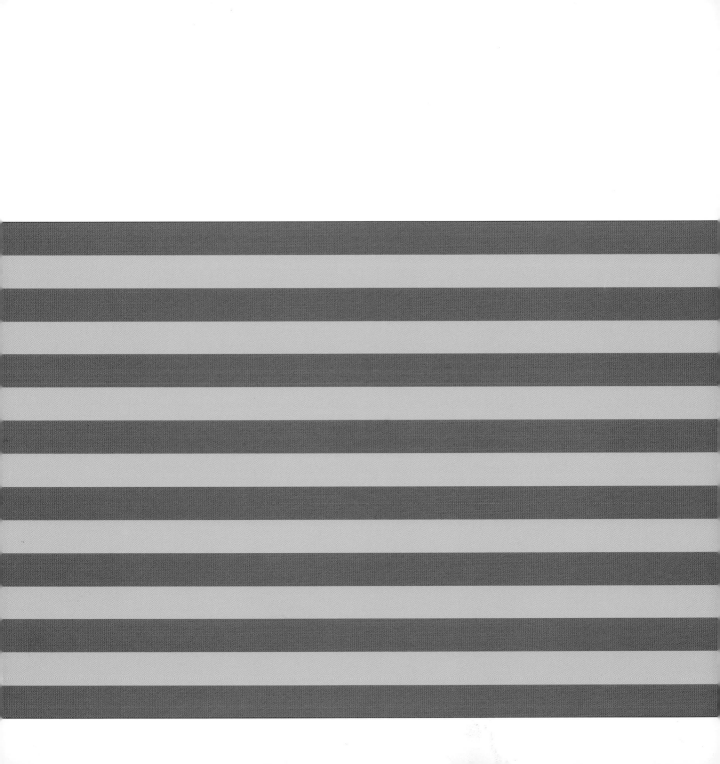

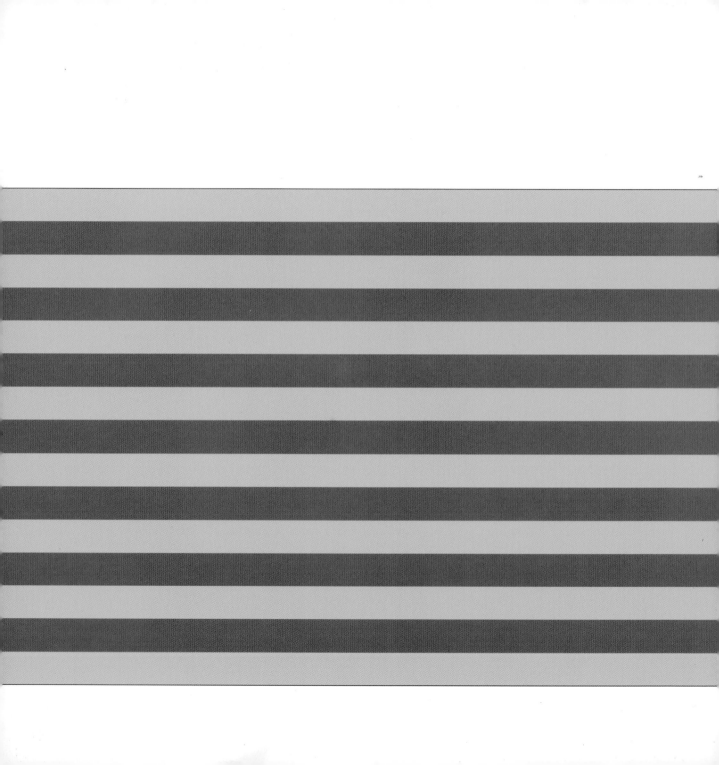

SANDWICH SPREADS, RELISHES, & TOPPINGS

Grainy Homemade Mustard

Toasted Nut Butter

Asian Peanut Sauce

Hot Jalapeño Mustard

Black Olive Tapenade

Mayonnaise with Fresh Herbs

Sun-Dried Tomato Pesto

Cilantro and Chipotle Pepper Pesto

Tropical Fruit Salsa

Horseradish and Caper Mayonnaise

Pear and Golden Raisin Chutney

Raita Cucumber Sauce

Vidalia Onion Marmalade

Avocado and Yogurt Sauce

Acar (Spicy Malaysian Pickle Salad)

Spicy Cocktail Sauce

Hummus Spread

Garlic Mayonnaise (Aioli)

Caper and Green Peppercorn Cream Cheese Spread

Gorgonzola Cream Cheese Spread

Garlic Herb Vinaigrette

Traditional Italian Pesto

Mediterranean Artichoke Salsa

Salsa Fresca

Green Olive Tapenade

Fresh Cranberry Orange Relish

Marinated Mushroom Salsa

Dilled Tartar Sauce

Tomatillo and Green Chile Salsa

Curried Mayonnaise

Roasted Red Bell Pepper Tapenade

Herbed Honey Mustard

GRAINY HOMEMADE MUSTARD

⅓ cup dry mustard such as Coleman's

¼ cup boiling water

2 tablespoons yellow mustard seed

1 tablespoon all-purpose flour

1 tablespoon brown sugar

¼ cup dry white wine

¼ cup white wine vinegar

2 tablespoons chopped fresh tarragon

⅛ teaspoon ground allspice

Salt and freshly ground black pepper

In a small bowl combine the mustard with the boiling water to form a paste. Let sit for 1 hour for the flavor to develop.

In a small saucepan over low heat, stir together the mustard paste, mustard seed, flour, brown sugar, dry white wine, and white wine vinegar. Simmer, stirring constantly, until the mixture has thickened, about 5 minutes. Remove from the heat and stir in the tarragon, allspice, and salt and pepper to taste. Cool, cover, and refrigerate for up to 2 weeks. Before serving, whisk the mixture until smooth.

TOASTED NUT BUTTER

½ cup salted peanuts

½ cup salted cashews

½ cup pecans

2 tablespoons butter

1 tablespoon peanut oil

1 tablespoon honey

1 tablespoon molasses

½ teaspoon Tabasco, or to taste

Salt and freshly ground black pepper

Preheat the oven to 400° F. Scatter the nuts on a baking sheet and place in the center of the oven. Toast for 6 to 8 minutes, or until the nuts are golden brown and aromatic, stirring occasionally.

Remove from the oven and allow to cool.

In a food processor grind the nuts until very fine. Add the butter, peanut oil, honey, molasses, Tabasco, and salt and pepper to taste. Process until smooth, about 2 minutes, scraping down the sides of the bowl as needed. Cover and refrigerate for up to 2 weeks.

ASIAN PEANUT SAUCE

1 tablespoon chopped fresh ginger

2 garlic cloves, finely chopped

⅓ cup crunchy peanut butter

2 tablespoons soy sauce

2 tablespoons rice wine vinegar

1 tablespoon dark Asian sesame oil

1 teaspoon honey

½ teaspoon red pepper flakes

Juice of 1 lime

2 tablespoons sesame seeds

In a small bowl whisk together all ingredients. Cover and refrigerate for up to 2 weeks.

HOT JALAPEÑO MUSTARD

¼ cup yellow mustard seeds

¼ cup apple cider vinegar

½ cup Dijon mustard

2 tablespoons dry mustard such as Coleman's

1 tablespoon honey

1 garlic clove, chopped

1 jalapeño pepper, seeded and finely chopped

Salt and freshly ground black pepper

In a small bowl whisk together all ingredients. Season to taste with salt and pepper. Cover and refrigerate for up to 1 week.

BLACK OLIVE TAPENADE

1 cup niçoise or kalamata olives, rinsed and drained,
   halved and pitted

2 anchovy fillets

2 garlic cloves, finely chopped

2 green onions, chopped

1 tablespoon capers, rinsed and drained

1 tablespoon herbes de Provence

¼ cup chopped fresh basil

⅓ cup extra-virgin olive oil

1 tablespoon freshly squeezed lemon juice

Freshly ground black pepper

In a food processor combine the olives, anchovies, garlic, green onions, capers, herbes de Provence, and basil. Process until the mixture is very finely chopped, scraping down the sides of the bowl as needed.

With the machine running gradually add the olive oil in a thin, steady stream until the mixture is very smooth, like a thick paste. Stir in the lemon juice and season to taste with freshly ground black pepper. Cover and refrigerate for up to 3 weeks.

MAYONNAISE WITH FRESH HERBS

½ cup mayonnaise

¼ cup sour cream

1 teaspoon Dijon mustard

⅓ cup assorted chopped fresh herbs such as parsley,
   basil, tarragon, rosemary, and thyme

1 tablespoon freshly squeezed lemon juice

1 teaspoon Worcestershire sauce

Salt and freshly ground black pepper

In a small bowl whisk together all ingredients. Season to taste with salt and pepper. Cover and refrigerate for up to 1 week.

SUN-DRIED TOMATO PESTO

MAKES 1 CUP

Juice and grated zest of 1 orange

⅓ cup oil-packed sun-dried tomatoes, drained

1 garlic clove, peeled

2 tablespoons seasoned bread crumbs

¼ cup freshly grated Romano cheese

¼ cup chopped walnuts, lightly toasted (see note on page 58)

2 teaspoons chopped fresh rosemary

⅓ cup extra-virgin olive oil

Salt and freshly ground black pepper

In a food processor combine the orange juice and zest, sun-dried tomatoes, garlic, bread crumbs, Romano cheese, walnuts, and rosemary. Process until finely chopped, scraping down the sides of the bowl as needed. With the machine running, gradually add the olive oil in a thin steady stream and process until smooth. Season to taste with salt and pepper. Cover and refrigerate for up to 2 weeks or freeze for up to 1 month. Stir well before using.

CILANTRO & CHIPOTLE PEPPER PESTO

MAKES 1 CUP

2 cups firmly packed cilantro leaves (about 2 bunches), washed and dried

2 garlic cloves, peeled

⅓ cup pine nuts (pignoli) or walnuts, lightly toasted (see note on page 58)

1 to 2 tablespoons chopped chipotles in adobo sauce

1 teaspoon ground cumin

⅓ cup extra-virgin olive oil

Salt and freshly ground black pepper

Place the cilantro leaves, garlic, pine nuts, chipotles with adobo sauce, and cumin in a food processor. Process until finely chopped, scraping down the sides of the bowl as needed. With the machine running, add the olive oil in a thin, steady stream and process until smooth. Season to taste with salt and pepper. Store in the refrigerator for 2 weeks, lightly covered with a thin layer of olive oil, or freeze for up to 1 month.

TROPICAL FRUIT SALSA

1 (15½ ounce) can unsweetened pineapple chunks, drained

2 kiwi fruit, peeled and cut into ½-inch dice

½ cup chopped red onion

2 garlic cloves, finely chopped

½ cup chopped walnuts, lightly toasted (see note on page 58)

2 tablespoons freshly squeezed lime juice

1 tablespoon soy sauce

1 tablespoon dark Asian sesame oil

⅓ cup chopped fresh cilantro leaves

2 dried chipotle peppers, reconstituted in water for 30 minutes, drained, and finely chopped

Salt and freshly ground black pepper

In a medium bowl toss together all ingredients. Season to taste with salt and pepper. Make at least 4 hours before serving to give the flavors a chance to mingle. Cover and refrigerate for up to 3 days. Serve chilled or at room temperature.

HORSERADISH & CAPER MAYONNAISE

½ cup mayonnaise

2 teaspoons Dijon mustard

2 tablespoons prepared horseradish

2 tablespoons capers

1 tablespoon chopped fresh parsley

1 tablespoon freshly squeezed lemon juice

1 teaspoon Worcestershire sauce

Salt and freshly ground black pepper

In a small bowl whisk together all ingredients. Season to taste with salt and pepper. Cover and refrigerate for up to 1 week.

PEAR & GOLDEN RAISIN CHUTNEY

2 tablespoons butter

1 red onion, chopped

2 tablespoons chopped fresh ginger

⅓ cup apple cider vinegar

⅓ cup dark molasses

2 pears, peeled, cored, and coarsely chopped

½ cup golden raisins

⅔ cup pecan halves, lightly toasted (see note on page 58)

½ teaspoon Tabasco

¼ cup chopped fresh parsley

Salt and freshly ground pepper

Melt the butter in a medium saucepan over medium heat. Add the onion and ginger. Cook for 5 minutes or until the onion begins to wilt. Add the apple cider vinegar, molasses, pears, golden raisins, pecans, and Tabasco. Cook for 10 minutes, or until the pears are just tender, stirring occasionally to prevent sticking. Remove from the heat, stir in the parsley, and season to taste with salt and pepper. Cool, cover, and refrigerate for up to 1 week.

RAITA CUCUMBER SAUCE

1 cucumber, peeled, halved lengthwise, seeded, and cut into ¼-inch dice (about 1 cup)

1 cup plain low-fat yogurt

1 tablespoon freshly squeezed lemon juice

1 tablespoon chopped fresh cilantro

1 tablespoon chopped fresh mint

1 tablespoon chopped fresh dill

2 green onions, chopped

Salt and freshly ground black pepper

Squeeze any excess moisture from the cucumbers with paper towels. In a medium bowl combine all ingredients, seasoning to taste with salt and pepper. Cover and refrigerate at least 1 hour before serving. Store in the refrigerator for up to 3 days.

VIDALIA ONION MARMALADE

MAKES ABOUT 1 1/2 CUPS

2 tablespoons olive oil

3 Vidalia onions, thinly sliced

3 garlic cloves, chopped

1/2 cup chopped pecans

1/4 cup balsamic vinegar

1 tablespoon bourbon, optional

1/2 cup chicken stock

1 tablespoon honey

1 tablespoon chopped fresh rosemary

1/2 cup freshly grated Parmesan cheese

Salt and freshly ground black pepper

Heat the olive oil in a large skillet set over medium heat. Add the onions, garlic, and pecans. Cook, stirring occasionally, until the mixture begins to caramelize and turn a deep mahogany brown, about 30 minutes. Stir in the balsamic vinegar, optional bourbon, and chicken stock. Cook until the liquid has evaporated, about 5 minutes. Remove from the heat and add the honey, rosemary, Parmesan cheese, and salt and pepper to taste. Cool, cover, and refrigerate for up to 1 week.

AVOCADO & YOGURT SAUCE

MAKES 2 CUPS

1 cup plain low-fat yogurt, drained of excess liquid

2 tablespoons freshly squeezed lime juice

2 garlic cloves, chopped

2 green onions, chopped

3 ripe avocados, peeled and cut into small chunks

1/2 teaspoon red pepper flakes

Salt and freshly ground black pepper

1/4 cup chopped fresh cilantro

In a food processor combine the yogurt, lime juice, garlic, green onions, half of the avocados, red pepper flakes, and salt and pepper to taste. Process until smooth. Add the remaining avocados and cilantro. Pulse the machine on and off just to mix. Do not overprocess. You want the sauce to have texture. Transfer the sauce to a medium bowl, cover, and refrigerate at least 1 hour before serving. Store in the refrigerator for up to 3 days.

ACAR
(SPICY MALAYSIAN PICKLE SALAD)

1 tablespoon peanut oil

1 cup coarsely chopped Napa cabbage or bok choy

1 carrot, cut into 2-inch matchsticks

1 zucchini, cut into 2-inch matchsticks

4 green onions, cut on the diagonal into 1-inch pieces

1 (1-inch) piece fresh ginger, peeled and julienned

⅓ cup rice wine vinegar

1 tablespoon fish sauce

2 tablespoons soy sauce

2 tablespoons sugar

2 tablespoons (or to taste) chili garlic paste

⅓ cup chopped fresh cilantro leaves

1 tablespoon chili oil

½ cup chopped salted peanuts

In a medium wok or 10-inch skillet heat the peanut oil over medium-high heat until sizzling. Add the Napa cabbage, carrot, zucchini, green onions, and ginger. Stir fry until crisp-tender, about 3 minutes. Add the rice wine vinegar, fish sauce, light soy sauce, sugar, and chili garlic paste. Bring to a boil, cover, and cook for 1 minute. Remove from the heat and stir in the cilantro, chili oil, and chopped peanuts. Transfer to a bowl, cool, cover, and refrigerate at least 4 hours to allow the flavors to marry. Refrigerate for up to 1 week. Serve chilled or at room temperature.

SPICY COCKTAIL SAUCE

¾ cup chili sauce or ketchup

¼ cup apple cider vinegar

2 green onions, chopped

2 garlic cloves, finely chopped

1 tablespoon freshly squeezed lemon juice

2 tablespoons soy sauce

2 tablespoons prepared horseradish

¼ cup chopped fresh cilantro leaves

Salt and freshly ground black pepper

In a small bowl combine all ingredients. Season to taste with salt and pepper. Cover and refrigerate for up to 1 week. Serve chilled or at room temperature.

HUMMUS SPREAD

2 garlic cloves, peeled
2 green onions, coarsely chopped
1 (15½ ounce) can chickpeas, rinsed and drained
1 tablespoon ground cumin
1 teaspoon chili powder
1 teaspoon ground coriander
1 teaspoon black pepper
1 tablespoon honey
1 tablespoon freshly squeezed lemon juice
1 tablespoon Worcestershire sauce
⅓ cup tahini (sesame seed paste)
⅓ cup sour cream
1 (10 ounce) package frozen chopped spinach,
    defrosted and squeezed dry
Salt

In a food processor combine the garlic, green onions, chickpeas, ground cumin, chili powder, ground coriander, black pepper, honey, lemon juice, Worcestershire sauce, tahini, and sour cream. Process until smooth, about 1 minute, scraping down the sides of the bowl as needed. Stir in the chopped spinach, and salt to taste. Cover and refrigerate for up to 1 week.

GARLIC MAYONNAISE (AIOLI)

½ cup mayonnaise
2 teaspoons Dijon mustard
3 garlic cloves, finely chopped
1 green onion, finely chopped
1 tablespoon chopped fresh basil
1 tablespoon freshly squeezed lemon juice
1 teaspoon Worcestershire sauce
Salt and freshly ground black pepper

In a small bowl whisk together all ingredients. Season to taste with salt and pepper. Cover and refrigerate for up to 1 week.

CAPER & GREEN PEPPERCORN
CREAM CHEESE SPREAD

MAKES 1 CUP

1 (3 ounce) package cream cheese, softened

½ cup sour cream

¼ cup freshly grated Parmesan cheese

2 tablespoons capers, rinsed and drained

1 tablespoon brine-soaked green peppercorns, rinsed
  and drained

1 tablespoon freshly squeezed lemon juice

1 teaspoon Worcestershire sauce

2 tablespoons chopped fresh basil

Salt and freshly ground black pepper

In a small bowl combine all ingredients. Season to taste with salt and pepper. Cover and refrigerate for up to 1 week.

GORGONZOLA
CREAM CHEESE SPREAD

MAKES 1 CUP

1 (3 ounce) package cream cheese, softened

¼ cup sour cream

2 ounces Gorgonzola cheese, crumbled (about ½ cup)

1 tablespoon freshly squeezed lemon juice

1 teaspoon Worcestershire sauce

1 garlic clove, chopped

2 green onions, chopped

Salt and freshly ground black pepper

In a small bowl combine all ingredients. Season to taste with salt and pepper. Cover and refrigerate for up to 1 week.

GARLIC HERB VINAIGRETTE

¼ cup red wine vinegar

1 teaspoon Dijon mustard

2 garlic cloves, chopped

1 shallot, chopped

½ cup extra-virgin olive oil

½ teaspoon salt

½ teaspoon black pepper

½ teaspoon sugar

¼ cup assorted chopped fresh herbs such as parsley, rosemary, basil, tarragon, oregano, and thyme

In a small bowl whisk together all ingredients. Taste and adjust seasonings with additional salt, pepper, or sugar. Cover and refrigerate for up to 5 days.

TRADITIONAL ITALIAN PESTO

2 cups firmly packed basil leaves (about 2 bunches), washed and dried

3 garlic cloves, peeled

⅓ cup pine nuts (pignoli) or walnuts, lightly toasted (see note on page 58)

⅓ cup freshly grated Parmesan cheese

⅓ cup extra-virgin olive oil

Salt and freshly ground black pepper

Place the basil leaves, garlic, pine nuts, and Parmesan cheese in a food processor. Process until finely chopped, scraping down the sides of the bowl as needed. With the machine running, add the olive oil in a thin. steady stream and process until smooth. Season to taste with salt and pepper. Store in the refrigerator for 2 weeks, lightly covered with a thin layer of olive oil, or freeze for up to 1 month.

MEDITERRANEAN ARTICHOKE SALSA

1 (12 ounce) jar marinated artichoke hearts, drained

1 (6 ounce) jar roasted red peppers, drained

½ cup pitted kalamata olives

2 garlic cloves, chopped

4 green onions, chopped

2 tablespoons chopped fresh basil

1 tablespoon chopped fresh oregano

1 tablespoon freshly squeezed lemon juice

⅓ cup crumbled feta cheese

Salt and freshly ground black pepper

In a food processor combine the artichoke hearts, roasted red peppers, and olives. Pulse to coarsely chop the ingredients. Transfer to a medium bowl and stir in the garlic, green onions, basil, oregano, lemon juice, feta cheese, and salt and pepper to taste. Let sit at room temperature for 1 hour before using to allow the flavors to mellow. Cover and refrigerate for up to 5 days.

SALSA FRESCA

3 ripe tomatoes, seeded and chopped

2 garlic cloves, chopped

1 onion, finely chopped

3 green onions, finely chopped

2 tablespoons peanut oil

1 jalapeño pepper, seeded and finely chopped

3 tablespoons chopped fresh cilantro

2 tablespoons freshly squeezed lime juice

Salt and freshly ground black pepper

In a medium bowl toss together all ingredients. Season to taste with salt and pepper. Let sit at room temperature for 1 hour before using to allow the flavors to mellow. Cover and refrigerate for up to 5 days.

Note: When you make this salsa, do all of your chopping by hand. Using the food processor makes the mixture too watery.

GREEN OLIVE TAPENADE

1 cup sliced green olives with pimientos

2 anchovy fillets

1/2 cup chopped walnuts, lightly toasted (see note on page 58)

2 garlic cloves, finely chopped

2 green onions, chopped

1 tablespoon capers, rinsed and drained

2 tablespoons chopped fresh tarragon

1/3 cup extra-virgin olive oil

2 tablespoons balsamic vinegar

Freshly ground black pepper

In a food processor combine the green olives, anchovies, walnuts, garlic, green onions, capers, and tarragon. Process until the mixture is very finely chopped.

With the machine running gradually add the olive oil in a thin, steady stream until the mixture is very smooth, like a thick paste. Stir in the balsamic vinegar and season to taste with freshly ground black pepper. Cover and refrigerate for up to 3 weeks.

FRESH CRANBERRY ORANGE RELISH

1 orange

1 lemon

1 cup fresh or frozen cranberries

1 Granny Smith apple, cored and cut into chunks

1/2 cup sugar

2 tablespoons finely chopped crystallized ginger

1/4 teaspoon ground allspice

1/2 cup chopped pecans, lightly toasted (see note on page 58)

Cut the orange and lemon into eighths and remove the seeds. Do not peel the fruit. Place in a food processor and process until very finely chopped. Transfer to a medium glass bowl.

Add the cranberries and apple to the food processor. Pulse until coarsely chopped. Stir into bowl with chopped citrus. Add the sugar, crystallized ginger, allspice, and toasted pecans. Stir until the sugar dissolves. Cover and place in the refrigerator for at least 1 day before serving to give the flavors a chance to blend. Refrigerate for up to 3 weeks.

MARINATED MUSHROOM SALSA

1 (8 ounce) jar giardinera (pickled garden mix), drained

1 (4 ounce) jar sliced mushrooms, drained

¼ cup pitted kalamata olives

¼ cup pimiento-stuffed green olives

1 small red onion, chopped

1 carrot, shredded

4 green onions, chopped

2 tablespoons chopped fresh basil

1 tablespoon balsamic vinegar

⅓ cup crumbled feta cheese

Salt and freshly ground black pepper

In a large bowl combine the giardinera, mushrooms, black olives, green olives, red onion, carrot, green onions, basil, balsamic vinegar, feta cheese, and salt and pepper to taste. Let sit at room temperature for 1 hour before using to allow the flavors to mellow. Cover and refrigerate for up to 5 days.

DILLED TARTAR SAUCE

¾ cup mayonnaise

1 teaspoon anchovy paste

1 teaspoon dry mustard such as Coleman's

1 garlic clove, chopped

2 gherkin pickles, chopped

2 tablespoons chopped fresh dill

1 tablespoon freshly squeezed lime juice

Salt and freshly ground black pepper

In a small bowl combine all ingredients and mix well. Season to taste with salt and pepper. Cover and refrigerate for up to 1 week.

TOMATILLO & GREEN CHILE SALSA

MAKES 2 CUPS

6 tomatillos, chopped

1 (4½ ounce) can chopped green chiles, drained

½ cup chopped red onion

2 green onions, chopped

2 garlic cloves, chopped

1 small cucumber, peeled, cut in half lengthwise, seeded and finely diced

2 jalapeño peppers, seeded and finely chopped

Juice of 1 lime

½ cup chopped fresh cilantro

Salt and freshly ground black pepper

In a medium bowl combine all ingredients. Season to taste with salt and pepper. Make at least 4 hours ahead to allow the flavors to mingle. Cover and refrigerate for up to 3 days. Serve chilled or at room temperature.

CURRIED MAYONNAISE

MAKES ABOUT ⅔ CUP

1 tablespoon mild or hot curry powder, preferably Madras

½ cup mayonnaise

¼ cup sour cream

1 teaspoon Dijon mustard

1 tablespoon freshly squeezed lemon juice

1 teaspoon Worcestershire sauce

Salt and freshly ground black pepper

In a small skillet set over medium heat, toast the curry powder until it becomes very fragrant and just begins to smoke, about 2 minutes. Be careful not to burn the curry powder as it will taste scorched.

In a small bowl, whisk together the curry powder, mayonnaise, sour cream, Dijon mustard, lemon juice, and Worcestershire sauce. Season to taste with salt and pepper. Cover and refrigerate for up to 2 weeks.

ROASTED RED
BELL PEPPER TAPENADE

2 roasted red bell peppers (see note), chopped

12 oil-packed sun-dried tomatoes, drained

2 anchovy fillets

2 garlic cloves, finely chopped

2 green onions, chopped

1 tablespoon capers, rinsed and drained

1 tablespoon herbes de Provence

¼ cup chopped fresh basil

⅓ cup extra-virgin olive oil

1 tablespoon freshly squeezed lemon juice

Freshly ground black pepper

In a food processor combine the roasted peppers, tomatoes, anchovies, garlic, onions, capers, herbes de Provence, and basil. Process until chopped. With the machine running add the olive oil in a thin, steady stream until the mixture is smooth and thick. Stir in the lemon juice and season to taste with the pepper. Cover and refrigerate for up to 3 weeks.

Note: To roast bell peppers, arrange the peppers on a grill rack or place them on a foil-lined baking sheet about 6 inches from the broiler. Roast until the peppers are charred all over, turning with tongs every few minutes, 5 to 8 minutes on the grill or about 15 minutes under the broiler. Place the blackened peppers in a heavy-duty zip-top freezer bag and seal. The steam will loosen the skin of the peppers. When cool enough to handle, gently remove the charred skin, tear open the peppers, and remove the seeds.

HERBED HONEY MUSTARD

½ cup coarse-grained Dijon mustard

⅓ cup honey

1 tablespoon chopped fresh rosemary

In a small bowl whisk together all ingredients. Cover and refrigerate for up to 2 weeks.

ACKNOWLEDGMENTS

Everyone plays different roles in this drama we call life. There are so many behind the scenes who offer to me their wisdom, guidance, creativity, good humor, support, friendship, and love. Thank you all for being a part of my life and helping to make this book possible.

Much love and appreciation are extended to the nucleus of my family life: my mom, Jan Overton; my brother, Ricky; my sister, Robyn; her husband, Tim; my nieces, Hope and Emma; my "Granny Lou"; and my "kids," Gypsy, Cagney, and Max. And special love and thanks to my dad, Ray "Bull" Overton. I know you are looking down and watching over me even as I write this. I hope I've made you proud.

To my editor, Sherry Wade, who came aboard toward the middle of this project. Thank you for making every process of this book a joy. I appreciate your understanding and look forward to many more projects together. Thank you, Burtch Hunter, who, with this book, has designed my last five. You are so very talented, and I am fortunate to have you on my team. And, once again, thanks to Chuck Perry, Steve Gracie, and Marge McDonald for continuing to support my writing endeavors. Also, I wish to thank my friend, Suzanne de Galan. As my former editor, you helped shape my writing style and were instrumental in picturing this book as part of a series. I wish you love and laughter.

Thank you to Brad Newton, my food photographer, who captured the essence of this book through his images. And to his assistant, Jaroslav Kanka, for helping to make the photo session run smoothly. I appreciate my new prop and food stylist, Angie Mosier. I thank you for the time and effort you put forth in making this book a success. It was a joy working with you.

I am grateful to Finn Schjorring and Faye Gooding of Le Creuset of America, Inc., for their support of my culinary projects, both with these books and the television production.

On a personal note I want to thank the friends of my inner circle (official taste-testers but unofficial food critics): Kay Ponder, Nancy McKenna, Kenny Conley, Brian Seifried, Stephen Barnwell, Jeff Eisenberg, Ken Folds, Clint Bearden, Susan Montgomery, Virginia Willis, and Nancy Rogers.

And, finally, to the nearly 10,000 students whom I have been able to entertain and teach over the years: Your enthusiasm and desire to learn is what made *Main-Course Sandwiches* a reality in the first place.

BIBLIOGRAPHY

Child, Julia. *The Way To Cook*. New York: Alfred A. Knopf, 1989.

Corriher, Shirley O. *CookWise*. New York: William Morrow and Company, Inc., 1997.

Craze, Richard. *The Spice Directory*. London: Quintet Publishing, Ltd., 1997.

Dupree, Nathalie. *Nathalie Dupree's Matters of Taste*. New York: William Morrow and Company, Inc., 1989.

_____. *Nathalie Dupree's Southern Memories*. New York: Crown Publishing Group, 1993.

Ferrary, Jeanette and Louise Fiszer. *Sweet Onions & Sour Cherries*. New York: Simon and Schuster, 1992.

Hadamuscin, John. *John Hadamuscin's Down Home*. New York: Harmony Books, 1993.

Herbst, Sharon Tyler. *The New Food Lover's Companion*. New York: Barron's Educational Series, Inc., 1995.

Jenkins, Steve. *Cheese Primer*. New York: Workman Publishing Company, Inc., 1996.

McGee, Harold. *On Food And Cooking*. New York: Scribner's Publishing, 1984.

Miller, Mark. *The Great Chile Book*. Berkeley, Calif.: Ten Speed Press, 1991.

Overton, Ray. *Layers Of Flavors*. Atlanta, Ga.: Longstreet Press, Inc., 1998.

_____. *Dutch Oven Cooking*. Atlanta, Ga.: Longstreet Press, Inc., 1998.

_____. *Main-Course Salads*. Atlanta, Ga.: Longstreet Press, Inc., 1999.

Revsin, Leslie. *Great Fish, Quick*. New York: Doubleday, 1997.

Ritchie, Tori. *Cabin Cooking*. San Francisco, Calif.: Weldon Owen, Inc., 1998.

Rombauer, Irma, Marion Rombauer Becker, and Ethan Becker. *The Joy of Cooking*. New York: Simon & Schuster, Inc., 1997.

van den Berg, Oona. *Toasted Sandwiches*. London: Hamlyn, 1998.

Willan, Anne. *La Varenne Pratique*. New York: Crown Publishing Group, 1989.

Worthington, Diane Rosen. *Picnics and Tailgates*. San Francisco, Calif.: Weldon Owen, Inc. 1998.

INDEX